Dōgen on Meditation and Thinking

Dōgen on Meditation and Thinking

A Reflection on His View of Zen

Hee-Jin Kim

State University of New York Press

Published by
State University of New York Press, Albany

© 2007 State University of New York

For information, contact State University of New York Press, Albany, NY
www.sunypress.edu

Production by Judith Block
Marketing by Susan M. Petrie

Library of Congress Cataloging-in-Publication Data

Kim, Hee-Jin.
    Dogen on meditation and thinking : a reflection on his view of Zen /
Hee-jin Kim.
        p. cm.
    Includes bibliographical references and index.
    ISBN-10: 0-7914-6925-5 (hardcover : alk. paper)—
    ISBN-10: 0-7914-6926-3 (paperback : alk. paper)   1. Dogen, 1200–1253.
2. Sotoshu--Doctrines.   3. Meditation--Sotoshu.   I. Title.

BQ9449.D657.K563 2006
294.3'927092--dc22   2006002192
    ISBN-13: 978-0-7914-6925-5 (hardcover : alk. paper)—
    ISBN-13: 978-0-7914-6926-2 (paperback : alk. paper)

10 9 8 7 6 5 4

For Jung-Sun

Contents

Preface

In recent decades, Dōgen's Zen has been relentlessly challenged by scholars of Dōgen studies, especially the proponents of Critical Buddhism within the Sōtō Zen academia who shook Sōtō orthodoxy to its core. Similarly, Zen Buddhism in general has been minutely scrutinized by a number of modern/postmodern Zen scholars, both within and without the Zen sectarian tradition. This scrutiny has involved issues ranging from the subitist (sudden enlightenment) orthodoxy to Zen folk religiosity, and from Imperial Way Zen to the reverse Orientalism of Nishida School philosophers.

Along with these challenges, Zen is experiencing a rude awakening from its spiritual hubris and cultural narcissism. It currently confronts an extraordinarily chaotic and fragmented world borne of the inexorable forces of science, technology, and global capitalism that have become increasingly misguided and dehumanizing, particularly following the demise of the communist world. We in the Northern Hemisphere—in sharp contrast to those in the Southern Hemisphere—are so materially affluent, so technologically advanced, and yet so morally and spiritually disoriented that we are at a profound loss as to how to manage such pressing issues as world peace, economic, social, and ecological justice, cultural and religious diversity, and the possibility of living authentically in today's world. Like other religious traditions, Zen cannot escape the exigency of this worldwide crisis.

Zen now stands at a crossroads. I submit that in such a contemporary context, Dōgen as meditator and Dōgen as thinker challenge us as much as we challenge him and his Zen. In this respect, we live in one of the most intellectually challenging and exciting periods in the history of the Zen religion and of Dōgen studies. Herein lies my desire to present this book with a sense of urgency.

In my previous book *Dōgen Kigen: Mystical Realist*, recently republished as *Eihei Dōgen: Mystical Realist*,[1] I endeavored in part to articulate salient aspects of Dōgen's methodology, including how he practiced his

Zen. I realized early on in my study of Dōgen that his sensibilities to, and his ways of dealing with, language, thinking, and reason were key to understanding and assessing the way he *did* his religion. It was, therefore, absolutely critical to uncover Dōgen's fundamental presuppositions of duality and nonduality, as they related to his religious methodology.

A few main points of my investigation were: (1) In contrast to the prevailing Zen tradition that had been founded upon an epistemological dualism between equality and differentiation, intuition and intellect, meditation and wisdom, Dōgen restored language, thinking and reason—the familiar tools of duality—to their fully deserved legitimacy in his Zen. At the same time, he never lost sight of their ultimate limitations, as well as the supreme importance of nonduality. (2) Nonduality in his view did not signify the transcendence of duality so much as the realization of it. The function of nonduality was not to efface duality, as often is the case with that of good and evil, nor to make duality a provisional expedient for attaining a *sui generis* experience, nor to plunge into ineffable reality. (3) Nonduality was always embedded and active within duality itself—as the guider, purifier, and empowerer of duality. The two were appropriated soteriologically, not theoretically or as explanatory concepts. And finally, (4) Dōgen's manner of approaching duality and nonduality was neither hierarchical, teleological, nor reified.

This present work offers some sundry results of my continued efforts to explore and explicate Dōgen's religious method along the aforementioned line of interpretation. I expand upon some issues and points from my previous work, amend others, and offer new observations, reflections, and analyses. In many ways, the present book complements and surpasses its predecessor. My textual analyses and critical reflections, though brief and schematic, center around such topics as original ambiguity inherent in both delusion and enlightenment, the meaning of negotiating the Way in Dōgen's praxis-oriented religion, the dynamic functions of emptiness as illustrated in the steelyard analogy, the realizational view of language, the notion of nonthinking/right thinking as the essence of seated meditation, and a multifaceted, radical conception of reason.

By discussing these subject matters in six short chapters,[2] I wish to bring Dōgen the meditator *and* Dōgen the thinker into relief. The focus of my investigation in this work is on meditation and thinking, an issue that has fascinated me since my first encounter with Dōgen in the late 1950s. More than anything else, however, I have tried to explore and understand the dynamics of duality as they relate to nonduality in the temporality of existence-time.

It has always been a personal delight and challenge for me as a scholar of Dōgen studies to find that such a traditionalist as Dōgen, who often reminded himself and his disciples of "holding the ancients in reverence" (*bōko*), read ancient writings and sayings in such a strikingly original and transgressive manner. For this reason, just as Confucius was famously characterized by Herbert Fingarette as a traditionalist *and* visionary,[3] Dōgen may well be regarded in a similar vein. Indeed, Dōgen seems to embody the qualification of the ideal teacher that Confucius had in mind when he said: "He who by reanimating the Old can gain knowledge of the New is fit to be a teacher."[4]

Dōgen "reanimated" the archaic tradition of meditation. It was a hermeneutic imperative for him to live on the boundary where ancients and moderns met and to engage them in dialogue. He now challenges us to do the same in a task that has no end. Perhaps that is the only way we can move beyond the ancients (including Dōgen himself), and ultimately move beyond ourselves the moderns (and postmoderns).

In view of this, throughout the present work, I situate myself methodologically and hermeneutically at the intersection of Dōgen's Zen and our contemporary crisis, in an attempt to facilitate mutual communication and understanding as empathetically and critically as possible.

I would like to extend my gratitude to the following people: Nancy Ellegate and the staff at State University of New York Press for making this publication possible; Soo-Jin Kim of Hallym University in Korea for his word processing expertise of glossary terms; Patricia Hall and Pearl Kim-Kregel for their editorial assistance at different stages of the project; and Patrick Charles for his word processing of early drafts. And finally, I thank my wife Jung-Sun for her moral support and immeasurable help throughout the entire project—the present work is dedicated to her.

Hee-Jin Kim
Eugene, Oregon
October 2005

Acknowledgments

Chapter 4 is adapted from "'The Reason of Words and Letters':Dōgen and Kōan Language" by Hee-Jin Kim, in William R. LaFleur, ed., *Dōgen Studies*, Kuroda Institute Studies in East Asian Buddhism, no. 2 (Honolulu: University of Hawaii Press, 1985), pp. 54–82, by permission of the press.

CHAPTER 1

A Shattered Mirror, a Fallen Flower

I

It is axiomatic in Zen Buddhism that delusion and enlightenment constitute a nondual unity (*meigo ichinyo*). For the sake of argument, let me formulate this dictum: Enlightenment is construed as seeing things as they really are rather than as they appear; it is a direct insight into, and discernment of, the nature of reality that is apprehended only by wisdom, which transcends and is prior to the activity of discriminative thought. In this view, delusion is defined as all that is opposed to enlightenment.

The problem with this reading is manifold: (1) There is an inherent tendency to bifurcate between "things as they really are" and "things as they appear to be"; (2) its corollary is that there is an unbridgeable chasm between insight/discernment and discrimination; (3) "seeing" is conceived predominantly in epistemological, intuitive, and mystical terms; (4) the pre- or extradiscriminative state of mind is privileged in such a way that creative tensions between delusion and enlightenment are all but lost; (5) nonduality in the unity is virtually the neutralization of all discriminations and thus has little or nothing to encourage and nurture duality as such—that is, discriminative thinking, intellect, language, and reason—in the scheme of Zen's soteriological realization; and (6) the implications for Zen discourse and practice, especially ethics, are seriously damaging. What we see here is a formulaic understanding—and misunderstanding at that—of the nonduality of delusion and enlightenment.

On the other hand, the ultimate paradox of Zen liberation is said to lie in the fact that one attains enlightenment only in and through delusion itself, never apart from it. Strange as that may sound, enlightenment has no exit from delusion any more than delusion has an exit from enlightenment. The two notions need, are bound by, and interact with one another. That said, the *interface* of delusion and enlightenment in their dynamic, nondual unity is extremely complex, elusive, and ambiguous. Since they are the two foci[1] of realization, we might ask how they interplay with one another. Should and can enlightenment overcome delusion? What does "overcoming" mean? In this chapter, I would like to examine aspects of how Dōgen treats delusion and enlightenment in their nonduality, with the foregoing pointers and issues in mind. In my view, Dōgen deeply delved into this profound mystery.

2

Consider the kōan Dōgen cites in his exposition on great enlightenment (*daigo*):

> A monastic once asked Great Teacher Pao-chih of the Hua-yen monastery in Ching-chao (a successor to Tung-shan; also known as Hsiu-ching): "What is it like when a greatly enlightened person is nevertheless deluded?" The teacher replied: "A shattered mirror never reflects again; a fallen flower never returns to the tree."[2]

Dōgen's praise and enthusiasm for this revelatory occasion is immediate and unreserved: "[This teaching] would never have been presented outside Hua-yen's assembly, nor could [Hua-yen] have provided such spiritual assistance had he not been Tung-shan's rightful [dharma] child. Indeed this [Hua-yen's assembly] was the dharma-seat of a fully realized buddha-ancestor!"

Traditionally, commentators by and large have taken Hua-yen's original kōan as representing the nonattached, self-emptying, traceless state of realization on the part of an enlightened one, who is thoroughly immersed in delusion and yet completely free of it. This conventional interpretation does not sufficiently address issues involved in the *dynamic interplay* of delusion and enlightenment, in their duality and nonduality. Why are delusion and enlightenment qualified as "great"? What is the meaning of being "nevertheless deluded" (*kyakumei*)? Why is it that a shattered mirror "never reflects again" and a fallen flower "never returns to the tree"? As I shall attempt to highlight in a moment, Dōgen's analysis of the kōan deeply penetrates the soteric dynamics of not only the nonduality, but also the duality of delusion and enlightenment.

Dōgen continues to comment:

> The greatly enlightened person in question is not someone who is greatly enlightened from the beginning, nor is the person someone who gets and appropriates it from somewhere else. Great enlightenment is not something

that, despite being accessible to everyone in the public domain, you happen to encounter in your declining years. Nor can it be forcibly extracted through one's own contrivances; even so, one realizes great enlightenment without fail. You should not construe nondelusion as great enlightenment; nor should you consider becoming a deluded person initially to sow the seeds of great enlightenment. A greatly enlightened person is further greatly enlightened, and a greatly deluded person is still greatly enlightened as well. Just as there are greatly enlightened persons, there are also greatly enlightened buddhas, greatly enlightened earth, water, fire, wind and space, and greatly enlightened pillars and lanterns. For now, the [monastic's] question is concerned about a greatly enlightened person. . . .

Consider this further. Is a greatly enlightened person who is nevertheless deluded the same as an unenlightened person? When being nevertheless deluded, does a greatly enlightened person create delusion by exerting that enlightenment? Or by way of bringing delusion from somewhere else, does the person assume it as though still deluded while concealing his/her own enlightenment? While an enlightened person remains the same in not transgressing his/her great enlightenment, does he/she, in any case, partake in being nevertheless deluded? Regarding "a greatly enlightened person is nevertheless deluded," you should also investigate whether the "nevertheless deluded" means fetching another "piece" of great enlightenment. And is the "great enlightenment" one hand and the "nevertheless deluded" the other? In any event, you should know that to understand "a greatly enlightened person is nevertheless deluded" is the quintessence of practice. Note that great enlightenment is ever intimate with the "nevertheless deluded."[3]

Earlier in his *Shōbōgenzō*, "Genjō kōan" (1233), Dōgen set out a broad outline of delusion and enlightenment: "For the self to carry itself forward and practice/verify the myriad things is delusion; for the myriad things to advance and practice/verify the self is enlightenment. Those who greatly enlighten delusion are buddhas; those who are greatly deluded about enlightenment are sentient beings. There are those who are further enlightened beyond enlightenment; there are those who are yet further deluded amid delusion."

Reflecting still further on these matters in the foregoing passages, Dōgen repudiates views of enlightenment as something one is innately endowed with, or as something to be acquired like things or objects, or as a fluke due to chance, luck, or fortune. The relationship between delusion and enlightenment is such that one is not the simple negation or absence of the other, nor does one precede or succeed the other. Enlightenment must neither descend to, nor incarnate as, delusion. It is, in Dōgen's favorite phrase, "ever intimate" (*shinzō*) with and transparent to delusion.[4] This intimacy (*mitsu*; *shimmitsu*) suggests the nonduality of delusion and enlightenment that, inasmuch as it always intimates lively tensions between the two, and precisely for that reason, makes enlightenment "*great* enlightenment" and delusion "*great* delusion" (*daimei*).

Delusion and enlightenment differ from one another perspectivally, are never metaphysical opposites (such as good and evil, or the one and the many, as ordinarily understood), and are both temporal, coextensive, and coeternal as ongoing salvific processes. In this respect, I would call them "foci" rather than "antitheses" or "polarities." They are orientational and perspectival foci within the structure and dynamics of realization (*genjō*). As such, their boundaries, though provisional, always remain and are never erased. Yet they are "permeable," so to speak, instead of "incommensurable." In light of such an intimate, dynamic relationship, enlightenment consists not so much in replacing as in dealing with or "negotiating" delusion in the manner consistent with its principles. By the same token, delusion is not ordinary by any means; it is constantly illumined and clarified by enlightenment in the ongoing salvific process, ad infinitum.

Parenthetically speaking, within the Zen soteric economy, any two foci are simply methodological designations and, as such, are nonsubstantial in having no independent self-nature. This also connotes that they are dependent on each other, along with all other terms and meanings involved in the whole context. In this empty, interdependent, and open context, foci are neither bifurcatory like metaphysical opposites in eternal struggle, nor do they collapse in the mystical coincidence of opposites (*coincidentia oppositorum*), nor are they polar principles that posit a preordained universal order or harmony above and beyond them. In short, foci are no more than the soteriological tools to guide practitioners in the dynamic workings of realization.

What is then the meaning of the "nevertheless deluded"? As I have observed before, there is no separation whatsoever of delusion and enlightenment. They are not strange bedfellows; on the contrary, they are working companions and need one another, with the shared purpose of actualizing salvific liberation. At this point, I suggest readers view enlightenment as radiant light that illumines delusion far and wide, just as moonlight illumines the earth at night. The radiant light penetrates and unfolds the depths and dimensions of delusion—in brief, human nature and the human condition—that have hitherto been unnoticed, unknown, or unfathomed by practitioners, who in turn become aware of their own emotional, existential, and moral anguishes, doubts and ambiguities. The illuminative and penetrating power of the radiant light can also be explained from the perspective of Dōgen's favorite statement: "Nothing in the whole world is ever concealed" (henkai fuzōzō). This is not to say that light eradicates darkness, and as a result, all things hitherto hidden become plainly visible. The reason is that originally nothing is hidden, and accordingly, light does not need to remove darkness. What light does then is to perpetually illumine and penetrate darkness's abysmal depths in the open-ended process of dialogue between light and darkness. This is the intimacy of light and darkness.

With this in mind, perhaps we can better understand Dōgen's following statement: "When the Dharma does not yet completely fill your body-mind, you think that it is already sufficient. When the Dharma fills your body-mind, you think that something is missing."[5] Paradoxically, the more deeply one grows in enlightenment, the more clearly one discerns one's own frailties and limitations. Expand your horizons from the personal to the social to the cosmic, and you will find yourself inextricably intertwined with all beings—all propelled by "the vast and giddy karmic consciousness" (gosshiki bōbō; bōbō gosshiki). We do not become deluded any more than we become enlightened, for we are originally deluded. This insistence is unequivocally stated in the key passage: "Great enlightenment is ever intimate with the 'nevertheless deluded.'" In light of the logic of the "ever intimate" we are now familiar with, "nevertheless deluded" may now be conceived as "ever deluded."

The intimacy in "ever intimate" never obliterates the dynamic, dialectical relationship of delusion and enlightenment in which they inform, challenge, negotiate, and transform one another. If Dōgen is mystical, his is the mysticism of intimacy, that is, in the sense of interplay, not adhesion or union. Enlightenment after all is to overcome delusion, by way of sensitizing practitioners to complexities and problems of the human situation. It is never free of values and meanings, and frustrations and disappointments any more than delusion is. Thus this caveat rings true:

> Therefore, the "nevertheless deluded" is not the same as mistaking a thief for one's son or one's son for a thief. Great enlightenment is recognizing a thief as a thief; to be "nevertheless deluded" is to recognize a son as a son. To add a little to a large amount is great enlightenment; to take a little from a small amount is the "nevertheless deluded." Accordingly, seek out and restrain someone who is "nevertheless deluded," and you will eventually encounter a greatly enlightened person. You should examine and act upon whether this present self is "nevertheless deluded" or not. This is the way you meet with the buddha-ancestors.[6]

Small "additions" and "subtractions"—those differences generated through practitioners' religious and moral efforts in changing circumstances—are due to the dynamic interaction of delusion and enlightenment. This is so because, according to the logic of intimacy, the differences between them are never erased, yet the hiatus between them is absent. Moral principles, values, and judgments are absolutely imperative in one's transformative life. This is why we should recognize "a thief as a thief" and "a son as a son," and never mistake one for the other. The differences matter; intimacy without them loses its identity as well as its efficacy. Dōgen warns us here against the slightest hint of antinomianism, relativism, and fatalism that might enter practitioners' thoughts upon hearing the ever deludedness of the enlightened one. It is for this reason that Dōgen insists: "'A greatly enlightened person is nevertheless deluded' is the quintessence of *practice*." A proper understanding of the insidiousness of delusion and the ambiguity of enlightenment thus constitutes the pivot of practice.

3

As is clear from the foregoing observations, "a shattered mirror" (*hakyō*) and "a fallen flower" (*rakka*) are the metaphors neither for a spiritually bankrupt person in despair and hopelessness, nor for an utterly incorrigible person beyond all possibilities of redemption. To the contrary, these metaphors purport to be the truth of realization vis-à-vis the existential predicament of the self and the world that are alike in a "shattered" and "fallen" state—not only figuratively but literally. For Dōgen, a figure of speech in the Buddha-dharma is itself ultimate reality.[7]

Nevertheless, why is it that "a shattered mirror *never reflects again*; a fallen flower *never returns to the tree*"? Dōgen has this to say:

> This teaching speaks of *right this moment* at which the mirror is shattered. It is not correct to imagine the time when the mirror is not yet shattered and thereby understand the words "a shattered mirror." The import of Hua-yen's present saying, "A shattered mirror never reflects again; a fallen flower never returns to the tree," might be interpreted in this way: Because a greatly enlightened person "never reflects again" or "never returns to the tree," he/she is no longer subject to any delusion. This, however, is not a proper understanding. If some think this, you might ask them: "What is the everyday life of a greatly enlightened person like?" In response, they will admit such a person is nevertheless deluded. The present teaching differs from all this: The question is "What is it like when a greatly enlightened person is

nevertheless deluded?" [The monastic] is inquiring about *right this moment of being nevertheless deluded.*

Such a moment is uttered as the realization of "a shattered mirror never reflects again" and "a fallen flower never returns to the tree." When a fallen flower is truly a fallen flower, even though it climbs beyond the top of a hundred-foot pole, it is still the fallen flower. Because a shattered mirror is truly a shattered mirror, even if it attains a certain degree of enlightenment in its daily living, its reflected light "never reflects again."[8]

The crux of Dōgen's interpretation consists in "right this moment" (*shōtō immoji*). It refuses to yearn for a paradisiacal state of enlightenment as a way of making sense of the "shattered" and "fallen" state. It does not atemporalize enlightenment so as to make it immune to delusion. Dōgen flatly rejects any manner of privileging enlightenment as opposed to, or as independent of, delusion, in causal, teleological, or metaphysical terms. Delusion has nothing to do with being prior to, posterior to, outside, or peripheral to, enlightenment. It always *co*exists with enlightenment, here and now. Note that the metaphoric vision of being "shattered" or "fallen" signifies the deeply unsettling human predicament that calls for practice right this moment—beyond any explanation, interpretation, or rationalization of it. Thus the urgency to live such a shattered and fallen state thoroughly and penetratingly in a given historical situation is critical.

"Right this moment" underscores the fact that enlightenment is as time bound and time free as delusion. In Dōgen's Zen, the realization of such thoroughgoing temporality and existentiality in which delusion and enlightenment are rooted is the foundation of its salvific project. In this context, "never reflects again" means there was no mirror in the first place that reflected and was then broken. By the same token, "never returns to the tree" is so because there was no tree of any kind from which a flower was fallen and to which it can presumably return. In this soteric economy, there remains only the reality/truth of a vision of the human condition at this very moment as "shattered" and "fallen." Hence, instead of offering the why, Dōgen simply takes the vision to be "the quintessence of practice."

Let me make a few further observations regarding the matter just discussed in the last paragraph. (1) The "never reflects again" and "never returns to the tree" should not be construed in the context of the Buddhist theory of the three ages of the right dharma, imitative dharma, and degenerate dharma (*shō-zō-matsu no sanji*), which was all too often tainted with a deeply fatalistic historical consciousness of romantic pessimism. Those expressions in question imply no nadir or stage in a devolutionary, let alone an evolutionary, scheme of things. Unlike other Kamakura Buddhist leaders such as Shinran (1173–1262) and Nichiren (1222–1282) to whom the doctrine was foundational to their religions, Dōgen dismissed it as irrelevant and ineffectual.[9] (2) Similarly, the "never reflects again" and "never returns to the tree," as I have briefly mentioned a moment ago, do not represent the state of total depravity in the sense of humanity entirely corrupted and incapacitated beyond redemption. Nor do they show a fall from an idealized or reified state of the "mirror" or "flower" (just as in the Fall of Adam and Eve from the Garden of Eden). Not that one falls from grace and is saved by grace in a theistic framework, but that, as Dōgen writes, "the one who falls because of the ground rises always because of the very ground" (*chi ni yorite taoruru mono wa kanarazu chi ni yorite oku*).[10] For better or for worse, both gravity and countergravity are firmly embedded in the ground itself. "Grace" is found within and around one's self, not outside it. And (3) the "never reflects again" and "never returns to the tree" do not refer to the situation to which some humans are predestined or doomed, as some Buddhists maintain in the doctrine of *icchantika* (*issendai*). Some humans may no doubt be enslaved and fettered by delusional conditions. But in Dōgen's salvific project that rigorously adheres to the doctrine of karma (*gō*), there is no agent or law that predestines a certain class of people to eternal damnation, nor are there sentient beings who are doomed to such condemnation.

Perhaps most noteworthy in Dōgen's analysis is this: The human condition is such that even if we overcome delusion, we cannot eradicate it. Thus Dōgen underlines the fundamental limitations and ambiguities of our moral and religious *overcoming*, namely, enlightenment. This is also the ultimate limitation of Zen as a religion.

Dōgen thus writes:

> This is not to say that being "greatly enlightened" is like becoming a buddha or that being "nevertheless deluded" is likened to the state of an unenlightened person. Nor should you think, as some people do, that [a greatly enlightened person] becomes like an unenlightened person again [as told in the bodhisattva doctrine] or that the original Buddha assumes manifested forms [in the world so as to save sentient beings]. Those people speak as though one overstepped [the bounds of] great awakening and then became a sentient being. For our part, however, we do not say that great awakening is overstepped or it is gone, or that delusion appears. Our view is not like theirs.
>
> Indeed, great enlightenment is elusive; being nevertheless deluded is elusive as well. There is no delusion that obstructs great enlightenment: You create "a half piece" of small delusion by exerting "three pieces" of great enlightenment. Thus the Himalayas are greatly enlightened by virtue of the

Himalayas; trees and rocks are greatly enlightened by virtue of the trees and rocks. The great enlightenment of the buddhas is such that they are greatly enlightened because of sentient beings; the great enlightenment of sentient beings is greatly enlightened through the great enlightenment of the buddhas. [Delusion and enlightenment, the buddhas and sentient beings] have nothing to do with before and after.

The great enlightenment now under consideration belongs to neither oneself nor others. It does not come [from anywhere], and yet it fills the watercourses and ravines. Although it does not go [anywhere, while its being nevertheless deluded], we should absolutely avoid seeking it elsewhere by acting with others. Why is this? Remember [the saying] "It will go along with the other."[11]

Delusion and enlightenment are both said to be "elusive" (*mutan*), which also means "bottomless." They are indeed bottomlessly elusive and elusively bottomless. As such, enlightenment never functions without delusion whereas delusion is never meant to be without enlightenment. Such nondual unity applies to the relationship between buddhas (and bodhisattvas) on the one hand and sentient beings (ordinary, unenlightened beings) on the other. In their nondual unity, the buddhas (and bodhisattvas) and sentient beings have "nothing to do with before and after" and, by extension, above and below, inside and outside, real and apparent. The buddhas (and bodhisattvas) do not descend, nor do sentient beings ascend; the former do not assume or put on the forms of the latter. In other words, only when the causal, hierarchical, and teleological pretensions collapse, do delusion and enlightenment as well as the buddhas and sentient beings, at last, function wholesomely as foci within the soteriological milieu.

All things considered, the distinction, differences, and tensions between delusion and enlightenment—and between the buddhas and sentient beings—exist without violating nonduality. What I have endeavored to present in the foregoing few sections is Dōgen's analysis of such differences and tensions—that is, duality, which reveals his realistic vision of human nature as thoroughly delusion ridden (as much as it is enlightenment laden). In this light, the notion of realization, often exalted and even ecstatic, should be informed and tempered by such an existential assessment of the human predicament.

4

Before I move on to another closely related aspect of the subject matter under investigation, let me state, as a reminder, that what I have been concerned with in this chapter is the nature and dynamics of realization (*genjō*) in Dōgen's Zen, with special emphasis on delusion in the nonduality of delusion and enlightenment. It is fair to say that, in Zen religion and scholarship, enlightenment has more often than not overshadowed delusion despite Zen's insistence on their nonduality. This lopsided view has unwittingly led to the aggrandizement and indulgence of enlightenment in one way or another. One of the most significant contributions made by recent Zen scholarship, in my view, is its stripping enlightenment of all traditional pretensions. In particular, the critique of the immediacy, purity, and universality of the enlightenment experience is at once devastating and salutary. After the Socratic aphorism, we might say that an unexamined Zen is not worth living—but then, in the same breath, add that an unlived Zen is not worth examining.[12] In this context, Dōgen's analysis of delusion is extremely instructive for understanding the nature and dynamics of practice that have been grossly overlooked by practitioners of Dōgen's Zen, as well as by scholars of Dōgen studies.

Having said this, let me turn to Dōgen's following thirty-one-syllable poem (*waka*) on impermanence:

Yo no naka wa	To what shall
Nani ni tatoen	I liken the world?
Mizutori no	Moonlight, reflected
Hashi furu tsuyu ni	In dewdrops,
Yadoru tsukikage.	Shaken from a crane's bill.[13]

This poem teaches a familiar Buddhist truth that the moon (Buddha-nature) is completely reflected in each and every one of the countless dewdrops (all things), without discrimination, namely one in all, all in one. The poem, as I see it, however, goes further than such a formulaic understanding exercised in the context of nature and impermanence. The complete reflection of the moon is "shaken"—each dewdrop has a full yet shaken reflection of the moon. In using the words *yo no naka* for "the world," Dōgen does not talk about just life in general but shows his own situatedness in the particular historical and cultural world of tumultuous Kamakura Japan (1192–1333) in which he lived and died. Especially significant is the fact that while critically rejecting the ideology of the age of the degenerate dharma (*mappō*), Dōgen nevertheless lived through the *reality* of *mappō*'s crisis situation, coupled with innumerable natural and social calamities and ruinous chaos and despair. In that milieu, he probed the vicissitudes of existence with a precise, minute eye. That is, Dōgen's sense of impermanence was inseparably interwoven with the *mappō*'s perilous actuality, as seen through a tremendous range of thoughts and emotions. His sense of impermanence was indeed thoroughly enmeshed in the realities of medieval Japan.

Impermanence for the Japanese in the medieval period was primarily steeped in religio-aesthetic feelings toward nature with its ever changing, shifting phenomena and objects such as the four seasons, mountains and rivers, flowers and birds. Human affairs and the gods and buddhas of the spiritual world were subsumed under such an affective view of nature. It is well known that the medieval Japanese found solace and inspiration in emotively identifying with the ephemerality of nature rather than in intellectually and morally understanding and coping with it.

Dōgen, on the other hand, although he could hardly resist the predilection to poeticize the beauty of nature, was concerned with impermanence as the conduit of soteric realization from his religio-philosophical perspective. He presented a starkly realistic assessment of existence and its ultimate reason (*dōri*), by addressing the issues of birth-and-death (*shōji*), existence-time (*uji*), the Buddha-nature of impermanence/the impermanence of Buddha-nature (*mujō-busshō*), and so forth. The world, natural and human alike, envisioned as karma laden, was at once temporalized and sacralized. As a result, Dōgen's view of impermanence, as fused with a crisis consciousness and its concomitant sense of urgency, was preeminently religious, moral, and existential, as compared with the general aesthetic view tinged with quiet, melancholic resignation.[14]

In light of the foregoing observations, Dōgen's poem may be paraphrased as such: "To what can I liken the human condition in which I live in the here and now? I say: 'The moon's *shaken* reflections in dewdrops.'" Consider this in the context of what we have observed in the previous sections on the nonduality of delusion and enlightenment. We now know that the moon's reflection in a dewdrop is not an ordinary reflection but is the moon itself, however shaken it is, and that the moon and the dewdrop are embodied as nondually one—temporalized and localized—in that shaken reflection. There is nothing but the shaken reflection in which shakenness and reflection are never statically/reductively fused, but dialectically/dialogically interactive. This is so neither by the moon's "descending" to the level of a dewdrop in order to be able to reflect, nor by the moon's "simulating" the form of reflection to identify itself with the dewdrop, but simply by the moon's being *intimate* with the dewdrop without violating either their duality or nonduality. This was precisely the meaning of *mujō-busshō* that meant not only "the impermanent are Buddha-nature" but also "Buddha-nature is impermanent." In this light, only when the moon is thoroughly temporalized and localized in a *particular* dewdrop, is the dewdrop genuinely sacralized as that shaken reflection. In this manner, Dōgen's poetic vision of impermanence in the image of the moon's shaken reflection in/as a dewdrop seems to unmistakably intimate elusive delusional undertones.

5

Dōgen delivered his talk on the radiant light (*kōmyō*) to his disciples at the Kannon-dōri Kōshō-hōrinji temple in the middle of a rainy night, one day in the sixth month, 1242. Utterly dark and quiet outside, it provided him with an opportune occasion to reflect on this important subject. This presentation now constitutes the *Shōbōgenzō*, "Kōmyō" (1242).

In this fascicle, commenting on Ch'ang-sha Chao-hsien's (n.d.) statement, "The entire world of the ten directions is one's own radiant light," Dōgen enunciates that one's own radiant light (*jiko kōmyō*) is not only the entire world of the ten directions (*jin jippōkai*) but also the buddha-ancestors' radiant light (*busso kōmyō*). In both instances, light is construed less as an attribute than as a function. That is, self/buddha-ancestor and light are coterminous and coeternal. The radiant light thus illumines the self and the world illimitably, leaving nothing hidden. As noted before, Dōgen's favorite expression "Nothing in the whole world is ever concealed" states exactly this situation. And as Dōgen writes, "There is no escape from this fact."[15]

Keeping these points in mind, let us examine Dōgen's comments on the saying by Yün-men Wen-yen (864–949):

> One day [Great Teacher Yün-men] addressed the assembly in the hall, saying: "Every person has the radiant light without exception. Yet when you look at it, you don't see it: Profound darkness. What is everybody's radiant light?" No response came from the audience. So he himself spoke for them: "The monastics' hall, the buddha hall, the kitchen pantry, the main gate."
>
> This Great Teacher's saying "Every person has the radiant light without exception" does not mean that the radiant light will appear in the future, or was in the past, or can be observed in the present. You should clearly hear what it says: "Every person *originally* has the radiant light." It is, as it were, assembling hundreds of thousands of Yün-mens in the hall and letting them recite the saying in unison. Yün-men's saying is not just his personal fabrication; it is what everybody's radiant light utters by exerting itself, in concert with and for the sake of others. "Every person has the radiant light without exception" thus means: *A whole person* originally has the radiant light; the radiant light *is* each and every person; everyone *exerts* the radiant

light in [his/her] personal and environing circumstances. [For this reason] the radiant light shines within everyone without exception; each [individuated] light originally shines within every person; everybody is authentically what he/she is; each [individuated] light is authentically what it is; every being is just as it is, through and through; and every wholeness is just as it is, through and through.

Therefore, you should know that the radiant light everyone has without exception pertains to each and every *actual* human being—that individual person within whom an individuated light wholly shines. Just ask Yün-men, "What do you mean by 'every person' and by 'the radiant light'?" Yün-men himself asked [in this vein]: "What is everybody's radiant light?" This question is none other than the radiant light itself, because it challenges its subject matter to the hilt. Accordingly, when anyone asks in such a manner, he/she has his/her own light.[16]

Why did Yün-men say, "Yet when you look at it, you don't see it: Profound darkness"? The key to the whole kōan seems to lie in a proper understanding of this puzzling statement. The metaphors of light and darkness are familiar in Zen as representing enlightenment and delusion, respectively. For one thing, if you try to see the radiant light as an object of perception, you will never be able to see it properly because it cannot be objectified in a dualistic manner. We must go further. In the *Pi-yen lu* (The Blue Cliff Record), Case 86, where the same kōan case appears, Yüan-wu K'o-ch'in (1063–1135) in his commentary offers a few pointers for exploring some subtle nuances. For instance, he cites the following verse by Shih-t'ou Hsi-ch'ien (700–790) in his *Ts'an-t'ung-ch'i* (Merging Difference and Identity):

Right within light there is darkness,
But don't see it as darkness:
Right within darkness there's light,
But don't meet it as light.[17]

In the same vein, Yüan-wu challenges by asking: "If you cut off light and darkness, tell me, what is it?" Or, he quotes a saying of P'an-shan Pao-chi (n.d.): "Light isn't shining on objects, nor do the objects exist. Light and objects both forgotten, then what is this?"[18] These pointers are correct in principle, suggesting the right direction to pursue; yet, they fail to point out, or to sufficiently explicate, the *dynamic relationship* of light and darkness.

Dōgen takes up the last-mentioned point explicitly in his foregoing commentarial passage. As noted before, there are some cues in his writings that amply suggest his dynamic praxis orientation with respect to this subject. Such notions as the "ever intimate" (*shinzō*) and "Nothing in the whole world is ever concealed" (*henkai fuzōzō*) should be recalled. I might add another of Dōgen's favorites: "As one side is illumined, the other is darkened" (*ippō o shōsuru toki wa ippō wa kurashi*). Additionally, let me quote the following in this connection that comments on a verse of Hung-chih Cheng-chüeh (1091–1157) in his *Tso-ch'an chen*:

> "[The essential activity of all the buddhas and the active essence of all the an-
> cestors] illumines without facing objects." This "illumination" means nei-
> ther illumining the outer world nor illumining the inner world; "without
> facing objects" is, as such, "illumination." Illumination is not transformed
> into objects, because the objects *are* the illumination. "Without facing"
> means: "Nothing in the whole world is ever concealed," or "Nothing issues
> forth when you uncover the world." Its meaning is subtle and mysterious, at
> once interrelated and not interrelated.[19]

Dōgen's logic here is clear: From the very beginning there is nothing hidden (or read substantial) throughout the world; therefore, there is nothing to be uncovered in the first place. In this sense, all things are clear as crystal (*rodōdō*). Inasmuch as light is always mediated by darkness, the function of light's illumination is to penetrate and see through darkness, not remove it. Accordingly, that perfect clarity of things—a vision, if you will—dif-fers from that reality/truth which has hitherto been hidden and is now uncovered. Rather, the vision as a focus is only the beginning, not the end, of the soteric process. Yün-men's "profound darkness" is the reminder of this fact.

For this reason, it is to be clarified ceaselessly through practice. How can you do this? First of all, the metaphysical opposites such as reality and appearance must go by way of the deconstruction of emptiness; they are simply ineffectual and inefficacious for soteriological purposes. In like manner, the notions of light and darkness must be first deconstructed by emptiness; only then can they function effectively, now reconstituted (or reconstructed) as salvific foci, through emptiness. As I shall explicate more in subsequent chapters, Dōgen's contributions primarily lie in the latter aspect of this dual role of emptiness, or in the treatment of duality in the pair of duality and nonduality.

Realization invariably consists of the ongoing interplay ("at once in-terrelated and not interrelated") of light and darkness, clarity and opacity, amid the nitty-gritty of the human situation. From this perspective, Dōgen suggests that light's illuminative power does not neutralize darkness to overcome it, but penetrates it so as to bring its hitherto unknown and unrecognized dimensions to daylight. In this way, light and darkness inform and transform one another in the salvific enterprise; the more light illumines, the more darkness is clarified. Enter Dōgen's view of delusion at this point, and you will see a rich amplification on Yün-men's "profound darkness." His words "bottomlessly elusive" (*mutan*) is also highly suggestive in this regard.

Against the background of these observations, Dōgen's analysis of Yün-men's statements becomes more comprehensible to us. As is clear from his commentary, Dōgen underlines the *individuated* forms of the radiant light, in their respective, unadulterated existentialities. Earlier in the fascicle he illustrates: "roots, stalks, branches, and leaves," "flowers, fruits, luster, and colors," "grasses and trees, walls and partitions," "mist and fog, streams and stones," "the bird's [traceless] path and the mysterious path [of enlightenment]," and so on. The radiant light has shapes, colors, sounds, and other myriad qualities and activities—not least important, human emotions, afflictions, passions, and suchlike—all are real in Dōgen's salvific world. Note that light does not become an individual being; each and every individual is light, a unique light at that. In other words, each being is *originally* an individuated light.

As I have observed elsewhere,[20] the radiant light for Dōgen is not a diffuse, universalized light so much as it is a confocal (with respect to light and darkness as binary foci), differentiated light, invariably local and temporal as a specific thing, being or phenomenon. In the former case, an individual forfeits its genuine identity and is absorbed into the universal light. In the latter, by contrast, an individual at once illumines and is illumined, reflexively, in its particularity, alive with its karmic conditions clearly discerned, in relation to all the other conditions. In short, the infinitely illuminative and penetrative power of the radiant light, be it at the macrocosmic or microcosmic level, becomes potent and efficacious only when localized and temporalized in concrete beings and situations. Only in that context can light not only break darkness but, more importantly for our purpose, penetrate darkness with the heightened awareness of its abysmal depths.

In this respect, the picture Dōgen offers here is neither that of light's conquest of darkness nor that of light's eternal struggle against darkness. Just as when enlightenment breaks through delusion, it is never outside that delusion, so light, however brilliant and dazzling, works always in and through darkness. It cannot be otherwise. This is why Dōgen writes: "Even though it is said, 'One is further deluded *amid* delusion,' you should construe it as saying, 'One is further deluded *beyond* delusion.' In such an understanding lies the path of progress in realization."[21] Replace "delusion" with "darkness," and you will have the same insight, now modulated from a different angle but still relevant to this section. This is the dynamic, dialectical notion of darkness. The upshot of this analysis then states: "*A whole person* originally has the radiant light; the radiant light *is* each and every person; everyone *exerts* the radiant light in [his/her] personal and environing circumstances." Dōgen's sole concern is after all soteriological and praxis oriented.

6

Dōgen's sensibilities to the peripheral, the obscure, the phantasmal, and even the seemingly irrational derive from his twofold concern: On the one hand, he was acutely aware of the immeasurable bounds and depths of the self and the world, the inner and the outer world, as contrasted to the fundamental limitations of human knowledge, even of "the measure of the buddhas" (*butsuryō*) and of "the measure of the dharma world" (*hokkairyō*). Despite or because of their epistemological limitations, humans have also the haunting awareness of their ultimate ignorance in the final analysis. This humility, however, never deterred Dōgen from opening himself up and exploring soteric possibilities with respect to the furthest reaches of the world and the innermost recesses of the self. In view of such humility and boldness in his methodology and hermeneutics, nothing is to be excluded from the purview of his soteriology.

On the other hand, Dōgen's sensibilities also stem from his cultural immersion in the Kamakura ethos of impermanence, inextricably intertwined with *mappō* (the degenerate dharma) culture and *hongaku* (original enlightenment) thought, full of chaos, despair, uncertainty, and unreason. In a world where madness and anarchy reign, the line between reason and unreason becomes extremely thin and blurred, and, as a result, one is naturally drawn to that ephemeral line's true colors. What is reason? What is unreason? How do we draw the line between them? Does the line still have any significance amid an anarchic world? I believe that Dōgen's sympathy with the deviant, displaced, and forgotten in the phenomenology of Buddhist experience, as observed in a different context elsewhere,[22] should be understood against the backdrop of Kamakura Japan.

Let me illustrate just one such case in point: In the *Shōbōgenzō*, "Kūge" (1243), Dōgen deconstructs a familiar Buddhist notion *kūge*, "flowers in the sky"—taken to be "illusory flowers" due to one's "dim-sightedness" (*ei*; *eigen*; *gen'ei*)—to read as "the flowers of emptiness." Dōgen is here adroitly making the most of another meaning of the Sino-Buddhist character *kū*, "emptiness," in place of its usual meaning, "the sky." While some Buddhists believe that dim-sightedness—the cataractous vision of the ordinary, unenlightened people—creates illusory flowers in the empty sky, and that only upon removing such dim-sightedness will those people be enlightened, Dōgen holds such a view is shortsighted. The truth, Dōgen argues, is that illusion and reality are nondually one. We are all familiar with this logic. And yet, in his characteristically original fashion, Dōgen now deeply probes the subtle workings of emptiness itself with respect to illusion and reality, delusion and enlightenment. For example:

> Never foolishly misconstrue dim-sightedness as falsehood and thereby look for truth outside it. That is a shortsighted view. If the flowers of dim-sightedness were false [on the assumption that truth is outside falsehood/dim-sightedness], the subject that misinterprets them as false and the objects that are misinterpreted as such would all be false. If all were after all false, truth could not be established. Without truth established, it cannot be the case that the flowers of dim-sightedness are false. Because enlightenment is rooted in dim-sightedness, all things that constitute enlightenment are invariably the ones adorned with the dim-sightedness. Because delusion is also rooted in dim-sightedness, all things that constitute delusion are invariably the ones adorned with the dim-sightedness, as well.[23]

Dōgen in this passage gives an incisive, effective refutation of what we today call the representational view of knowledge in which the mind is presumed to represent the reality existing independently of it, through perception, thinking, and language. Truth in this view is established in terms of a correspondence between mind and reality. Those who are familiar with Dōgen's Zen may not be surprised to see his foregoing commentarial statements, but what distinguishes him here is this: Without frontally taking on the doctrinal issue of the ultimate truth and worldly truth of Mādhyamika thought, and even by bypassing the doctrine as such, Dōgen elucidates the interior workings of emptiness itself. By minutely observing simple expressions such as *kūge* and *eigen*, he boldly declares that emptiness, along with delusion and enlightenment, is rooted in dim-sightedness.

Dim-sightedness highlights fundamental ambiguity and opacity—never neutrality or freedom from value-ladenness—as intrinsic to human knowledge and understanding, and even to what we legitimately claim to be reality and truth. If I may borrow the locution of Blaise Pascal (1623–1662) at this point who wrote, "Men are so necessarily mad, that not to be mad would amount to another form of madness,"[24] Dōgen's view runs like this: "Humans are so necessarily dim-sighted, that not to be dim-sighted would amount to another form of dim-sightedness." Such being the case, what the opponents of this view fail to realize is that their opposing assertion is itself none other than the product of dim-sightedness. Thus, their thesis is disastrously undiscerning and ill-considered; they are never able to establish any reality or truth outside the purview of dim-sightedness.

By contrast, according to Dōgen, this *original* dim-sightedness serves as the methodological and hermeneutic base of operation for his Zen soteriology; yet he avoids falling into positivist, reductionist, and relativist pitfalls. Dōgen, for instance, never minimizes nor erases the tensions between truth and falsehood. In this way, dim-sightedness is the life force of emptiness and, doctrinally speaking, is the linchpin of ultimate truth and worldly truth. "*Seeing* things as they are"—or "seeing things clearly"—will never be the same after one hears Dōgen's dim-sightedness.

Given all this, the illuminative, penetrative power of the radiant light now brings dim-sightedness into sharp relief, with equal force and eloquence as in "Nothing in the whole world is ever concealed." Dim-sightedness is no longer a physiological defect or a medical problem of faulty eyesight. It is not something to be cured or eliminated, but rather something to live out authentically. It is a salvific focus in the human condition, as original as enlightenment. "[Some unenlightened scholars] only think that the flowers seen in the sky (*kūge*) are due to faulty eyesight (*gen'ei*)," writes Dōgen. "But they do not understand that dim-sightedness (*gen'ei*) is what it is by virtue of the flowers of emptiness (*kūge*)."[25] "[All the buddhas] let their visions (*gen*) realize through dim-sightedness (*ei*). They realize the flowers of emptiness in their visions, and their visions in the flowers of emptiness."[26] With this deconstructive/reconstructive metamorphosis in the meanings of *kūge* and *gen'ei/eigen* at Dōgen's hand, dim-sightedness is at once liberated and radicalized in his soteric scheme.

Dōgen further writes:

> For these reasons we now say as follows: Just as dim-sightedness is equal, the flowers of emptiness are equal. Just as dim-sightedness is birthless, the flowers of emptiness are birthless. Just as all things are themselves ultimate reality, the flowers of dim-sightedness are ultimate reality. [The flowers of dim-sightedness/the flowers of emptiness] are not concerned with the past, present and future, nor with the beginning, middle and end. Because they

are not obstructed by arising and perishing, they freely cause arising and perishing to arise and perish. They arise and perish in *emptiness*; they arise and perish in *dim-sightedness*; and they arise and perish amid *flowers*. They are like this at all times and in all places.[27]

Considering the tumultuous world of his times and the incredible follies and madness of human beings, did Dōgen discern deeply perplexing, perhaps insoluble contradictions, in the inner dynamics of the duality and nonduality of delusion and enlightenment? My sense is that he went as far as he could in his exploration of those obscure, elusive dimensions of opacity and ambiguity in practitioners' realization that were nonetheless part and parcel of the Buddha-dharma. However advanced in realization, practitioners cannot escape this dim-sightedness, and yet, it is at the same time deemed to be an occasion for liberation, by virtue of emptiness. Thus equating dim-sightedness to emptiness, which I think is one of his most seminal insights into the temporality and existentiality of human nature, Dōgen envisions its flowers blooming as all things of the self and the world—rootless, birthless, purposeless. Dim-sightedness/emptiness does not lend itself to explanations, interpretations, and purposes. It only prompts practice in realization.

7

In this chapter, I have endeavored to elucidate Dōgen's understanding of the inner workings of delusion and enlightenment, light and darkness, illusion and reality, in their duality and nonduality. In his Zen, these binary foci were thoroughly temporalized from the perspective of impermanence, intensified by the consciousness of crisis and exigency, and radicalized by *hongaku* thought. As a result, the hitherto obscured dimensions of delusion and enlightenment, especially of the former, were accentuated as never before. Skillfully delving into those traditional notions, Dōgen argued (1) that humans had no exit from the "shattered" and "fallen" state of their delusory conditions; (2) that the illuminative power of the radiant light intensified, rather than neutralized, the heightened awareness of (individual and collective) delusional darkness; and (3) that dim-sightedness was the primordial condition of human knowledge and understanding, of thoughts and imagination, and of reality and truth. Delusion and enlightenment alike were ineluctably embedded in this condition. Such insistence was a far cry from acceding to nihilism, relativism, or cynicism, but a call for moral and spiritual endeavors with renewed vigor.

And yet, popular views persist, such as: (1) The enlightened one is *in*, but not *of*, the world of delusion; (2) inasmuch as the enlightened one is liberated, he/she is no longer affected by delusion; (3) enlightenment is sufficiently powerful so as to "burn off" karmic effects; and (4) only when enlightenment frees itself of delusion, does it attain its total purity. All sound fine and are admirable. What we have thus far seen in the present chapter—and will see in what follows—clearly disputes such smug views. After all is said and done, the enlightened one is a profoundly ambiguous, complex person, and Dōgen would not have excepted himself in this respect.

It should be noted further that while undoubtedly indebted to the *hongaku* thought of medieval Japan, Dōgen's religion perhaps reflects certain sentiments—on the dark side of the human psyche—akin to consciousness-only thought (*yuishiki shisō; Vijñāna-vāda/Vijñapti-mātratā*), which was transmitted in the Hossō sect in Japan.[28] We here glimpse his eclecticim.

CHAPTER 2

Negotiating the Way

I

In the *Shōbōgenzō*, "Bendōwa" (1231), Dōgen succinctly enunciates his Zen: "The endeavor to negotiate the Way (*bendō*), as I teach now, consists in discerning all things in view of enlightenment, and putting such a unitive awareness (*ichinyo*) into practice in the midst of the revaluated world (*shutsuro*)."[1] This statement clearly sets forth practitioners' soteriological project as *negotiating the Way* in terms of (1) discerning the nondual unity of all things that are envisioned from the perspective of enlightenment and (2) enacting that unitive vision amid the everyday world of duality now revalorized by the enlightenment. Needless to say, these two aspects refer to practice and enlightenment that are nondually one (*shushō ittō; shushō ichinyo*).

It may be instructive for us to note that the meaning of the term *shō*, which I have translated above as "enlightenment," has some important nuances as compared with other kindred terms such as *go* and *kaku*. The three Sino-Buddhist characters, *go*, *kaku,* and *shō*, are read as *satori* in the native Japanese way; the word *satori*, translated as "enlightenment," has become a household word in the West, thanks to D. T. Suzuki. Very briefly, *go* is often used with *mei* as in *meigo* ("delusion and enlightenment"), thereby stressing emancipation from delusions through insight into the true nature of reality or thusness (*shinnyo*). Its emphasis on intuitive apprehension by transcendent wisdom is quite clear. *Kaku* connotes the awakening of the mind from its spiritual slumber and therein an awakening to a hitherto unknown reality/truth; in this sense it is sometimes paired with dream (*mu*). By contrast, *shō* (which means "to prove," "to bear witness to," "to verify") signifies the direct, personal verification of salvific reality/truth through the body-mind (*shinjin*), one's whole being. A crucially important point here is, namely, "that which verifies" and "that which is verified" are inseparably intertwined via the body-mind. In this context, *shō* is typically coupled with *shu* ("practice") as in *shushō* ("practice and enlightenment"). Although *go, kaku,* and *shō* are used interchangeably in Zen Buddhism, as well as in Dōgen, his most-favored term is undoubtedly *shō.* Thus, in speaking of enlightenment (*shō*), Dōgen always presupposes *the process of verification* in which enlightenment entails practice, and vice versa. To put it differently, enlightenment (nonduality) makes it incumbent upon practitioners to put the unitive vision of all things into practice, in terms of duality of the re-visioned world.

In view of the famous putative question attributed to a young Dōgen on Mt. Hiei by his biographers of the Sōtō Zen tradition,[2] and which may very well have been prompted by unsettling implications of original enlightenment thought (*hongaku shisō*), we see that Dōgen frames his religion not so much in terms of whether to practice, but rather *how to practice.* How can practitioners authentically negotiate the Way in a specific daily situation, or in what Dōgen calls "a dharma-situation" (*hōi*)? This was the question Dōgen pursued throughout his monastic life.

Consider this additional statement by Dōgen: "A Buddhist should neither argue superiority or inferiority of doctrines, nor settle disputes over depth or shallowness of teachings, but only be mindful of authenticity or inauthenticity of practice." The above statement was part of Dōgen's response to his disciple's challenging question:

> Both the Hokke and Kegon schools that exist in our country today represent the ultimate teaching of the Mahāyāna. Furthermore, the teachings of the Shingon school, ever since their direct transmission from Vairocana Buddha to Vajrasattva, have been handed down from master to disciple, without interruption. Espousing "The mind itself is Buddha" and "This very mind attains buddhahood," the school also teaches that the Five Buddhas' true enlightenment can be attained in a single sitting, without going through many kalpas of spiritual discipline. It might be regarded as the most sublime form of the Buddha-dharma. In view of all this, the practice you advocate now—what advantages make you recommend it exclusively, while ignoring all other practices?[3]

The question here is vitally important not only because it queries Dōgen's assertion on the exclusive practice—or even superiority, as some might bluntly suggest—of seated meditation (*zazen*), but also because it refers to the Hokke (Tendai), Kegon, and Shingon schools of medieval Japanese Buddhism. In this context, mention of the doctrines of "The mind itself is Buddha" (*sokushin zebutsu*) and "This very mind attains buddhahood" (*zeshin sabutsu*) is quite significant, since they are the equivalents of the cardinal Shingon tenet, "This very body is the realization of buddhahood" (*sokushin jōbutsu*), which, along with other kindred notions, contributed to the developments of medieval (Tendai) *hongaku* thought referenced a moment ago. Advocating the absolute affirmation of the phenomenal world, *hongaku* thought was regarded as the zenith of Mahāyāna thought at one extreme, and the disclaimer of moral and spiritual efforts at the other. Against this background, Dōgen's foregoing answer stands out in its unequivocal praxis orientation.

Then what constitutes the authenticity of practice? To put it in the simplest terms, it has to do with the manner and quality of negotiating the Way through the dynamic, dialectical relationship of practice and enlightenment as two foci in the soteric context of realization (*genjō*).

2

Let us examine the last statement in some detail. Dōgen's view on the nondual unity of practice and enlightenment is paradigmatically stated:

> The view that practice and enlightenment are not one is a non-Buddhist view. In the Buddha-dharma they are one. Inasmuch as practice is based on enlightenment, the practice of a beginner is entirely that of original enlightenment. Therefore, in giving the instruction for practice, a Zen teacher should advise his or her disciples not to seek enlightenment apart from practice, for practice itself is original enlightenment. Because it is already enlightenment of practice, there is no end to enlightenment; because it is already practice of enlightenment, there is no beginning to practice.[4]

Other kindred expressions such as "original enlightenment and wondrous practice" (*honshō myōshu*), "practice and enlightenment are undefiled" (*fuzenna no shushō*), and so on, all reinforce the notion of the practice-enlightenment unity.

The prototype for the unity of practice and enlightenment, as all Dōgen students know, is "zazen-only" (*shikan taza*). In a nutshell, it consists of four aspects: (1) It is that seated meditation which is objectless, imageless, themeless, with no internal or external devices or supports, and is nonconcentrative, decentered, and open-ended. Yet it is a heightened, sustained, and total awareness of the self and the world. (2) It seeks no attainment whatsoever, be it enlightenment, an extraordinary religious experience, supernormal powers, or buddhahood, and accordingly, is non-teleological and simply ordinary. (3) It is "the body-mind cast off" (*shinjin datsuraku*) as the state of ultimate freedom, also called "the *samādhi* of self-fulfilling activity" (*jijuyū zammai*). And (4) it requires single-minded earnestness, resolve, and urgency on the part of the meditator.

Let me try, at this juncture, to articulate some structural aspects of the unity in question. This unity does not mean that practice and enlightenment, though originally two different realities or ontological antitheses, are merged into one, or are reduced to one or the other in a mystical union of numerical oneness or an uneasy alliance. Practice and enlightenment are neither the two complementary (and opposite) sides of the same reality, nor in a relationship of the periphery and the center. Neither are they related in terms of the surface and the core. To put it another way, the unity is not the nullification of differences between the two, nor is it a transformation of one into the other, or a fusion of one with the other. Practice and enlightenment are different, yet not two. Dialectical nonduality does not deny the *differences* between the two.

A unitary relationship between practice and enlightenment, furthermore, is not like the seed and the fruit, cause and effect, premise and conclusion, the means and the end, worldly truth and ultimate truth, or the kataphatic and the apophatic. Practice is neither a condition for, a stepping stone, or a means to enlightenment; on the other hand, enlightenment is not the result, reward, or goal of practice. Practice neither antecedes nor anticipates enlightenment; practice neither faces nor awaits enlightenment. Nor do the efforts and merits of practice cumulate in enlightenment. Enlightenment is not ontologically or epistemologically privileged over practice; it never lives in complete and serene independence of practice. Enlightenment is not *sui generis* or *causa sui*.

There is no path or linkage whatsoever from practice to enlightenment, and vice versa. In fact, they have nothing to do with each other so far as they are seen in logical, causal, teleological, epistemological, ontological, and similar frameworks. From Dōgen's perspective, even the bodhisattva's path of ascent and descent—"seeking enlightenment above, saving sentient beings below" (*jōgu-bodai geke-shujō*), as so eloquently espoused in Mahāyāna Buddhism—would be regarded as ultimately misleading.[5] In the end, the collapse of all sequential, teleological, hierarchical, and central-peripheral frameworks is complete and final. Dōgen's Zen arises in the ruins of such a collapse.

What I have belabored to say in the foregoing few paragraphs, at the risk of truism and tedium is (1) to provide my rationale in part for using "foci," not "antitheses" or "polarities," in order to better understand such notions as practice and enlightenment in Dōgen's Zen, and (2) to suggest that, despite Critical Buddhists' contentions—which I shall discuss in detail later—such as their claim that the early Dōgen was inconsistent and wavering in his treatment of *hongaku* thought,[6] Dōgen's overriding concern in discussing practice and enlightenment was *the quest for authentic practice.* This concern was a running thread throughout his monastic career. For this reason, he never atemporalized enlightenment by converting its supposed nonduality into a pure consciousness or an apophatic reality that negated any and all conceptual and symbolic mediations. In other words, although enlightenment for Dōgen was a total vision of the self and the universe, that vision did not and should not entail the universalistic legislation of its truth-claim as the only truth, because such a move would amount to a violation of Dōgen's perspectivally oriented logic of temporality.

Dōgen writes: "[The duality of] practice and enlightenment is not nonexistent, but cannot be defiled."[7] Elsewhere, he states: "[The nonduality of] practice and enlightenment is not undefiled [from the beginning]; its undefiledness, however, is not nonexistent."[8] In these two statements, Dōgen explicitly underscores, on the one hand, that while the duality of practice and enlightenment is in process, practitioners can make it undefiled by way of authentication by the nonduality, and on the other, that because this nonduality is never a given, practitioners must strive to realize it through the duality of authentic practice. That is to say, the undefiledness of practice and enlightenment always consists of the dynamic, dialectical relationship between them, as well as between duality and nonduality, and accordingly, has to do with the quality of such an interaction. The reciprocal verification of practice and enlightenment invariably takes place in a dynamic such as this.

The unity of practice and enlightenment as two foci, in this view, should never default on the communion and dialogue between them in a specific existentiality of practitioners' life situation, which Dōgen's "vast and giddy karmic consciousness" (*gosshiki bōbō, bōbō gosshiki*), for instance, vividly accentuates. Thus, Dōgen refuses to privilege or reify the unity in question by exercising an epistemological leap into it in the name of transcendent wisdom, as if such a move would spontaneously and instantaneously enable one to execute morally indubitable acts, as we see in some Zen extremists' arguments. The latter position would have been flatly repudiated by Dōgen as akin to "the naturalist heresy" (*jinen gedō, tennen gedō*) that supported the spontaneous generation of all things without causation—and hence by extension, enlightenment without any religious effort.

Furthermore, such thinking on the part of Dōgen seems to have been the reason for his disfavor of the theory of the two truths, in which ultimate truth was more often than not privileged over worldly truth. Candrakīrti's Prāsaṅgika Mādhyamika philosophy, according to C. W. Huntington, Jr., holds the incommensurability of the two truths: One "clashes with" but does not "contradict" the other. The worldly truth—our everyday experience through the normal ways of perceiving and thinking—is no more than a launching pad, so to speak, for plunging into the ultimate truth, in which all rational and conceptual contents ("the screen") of the worldly truth are stripped away.[9] In this interpretation, rational and conceptual contents have no soteriological significance except for a pragmatic one. From Dōgen's perspective, the so-called two truths should be thoroughly temporalized as a pair of foci within the dynamics of realization.

In view of the foregoing consideration, the lived relationship between practice and enlightenment in terms of the *not-nonexistent aspect* of their duality is an imperative in Dōgen's Zen. It involves painstaking, critically reflective processes of realization, by negotiating the Way amid the nitty-gritty of the human condition. Aside from this, Dōgen insists there are no genuine salvific possibilities. At the same time, such a relationship in terms of the *undefiled aspect* of nonduality renounces any privilege over the not-nonexistent aspect and thereby declares its identity as "not undefiled [from the beginning]." To put it another way, the undefiledness in question has to do with the process, not the state, of realization; it is a soteric vision, not a metaphysical principle. Note this notion goes beyond that of nonattachment, which has been so highly popularized in Zen discourse and practice. Thus, Dōgen endeavored to explicate and deepen the dynamic workings of such undefiledness throughout his monastic career.

3

One of Dōgen's favorite stories has to do with "Nan-yüeh's tile polishing."

> When Chiang-si Ma-tsu formerly studied under Nan-yüeh [Huai-jang], Nan-yüeh personally granted the seal of the mind to him. This is the beginning of [the tradition of] tile polishing. Subsequently, Ma-tsu resided in the Ch'uan-fa yüan, doing zazen daily for some ten years. We are told that, even when snowbound, he never neglected his practice, no matter how frozen his sitting place. One day when Nan-yüeh visited Ma-tsu's hut, Ma-tsu attended to him. Nan-yüeh asked: "What have you been doing lately?" Ma-tsu replied: "These days I am just doing zazen." Nan-yüeh: "What is doing zazen for?" Ma-tsu: "I strive to make a buddha." Then Nan-yüeh picked up a tile and began to polish it against a rock near Ma-tsu's hut. Seeing this,

Ma-tsu immediately asked: "Reverend, what are you doing?" Nan-yüeh: "I am polishing a tile." Ma-tsu: "What is polishing a tile for?" Nan-yüeh: "I am going to make a mirror by polishing it." Ma-tsu: "How can you make a mirror by polishing a tile?" Nan-yüeh: "How can you make a buddha by doing zazen?"[10]

A clue to the proper understanding of this kōan can be found in the opening sentences in which Dōgen refers to Ma-tsu as an accomplished teacher equal to Nan-yüeh's stature, and by implication, he suggests the story should be treated as a dialogue between two authoritative teachers, not between a teacher and his student.

According to some traditional interpretations, Nan-yüeh's final retort implies an unbridgeable chasm between meditation (*jō; dhyāna*) and wisdom (*e; prajñā*), and hence is a dismissal, or at best devaluation, of meditation in favor of wisdom. It is well known that Zen Buddhists have engaged in this issue throughout Zen history up until the present day—for the most part in terms of the official ideology of subitism (sudden enlightenment).[11] As for Dōgen, he offers as usual his own unorthodox conclusion:

Nan-yüeh says, "How can you make a buddha by doing zazen?"
    We now know clearly the truth that zazen does not await buddha making. Its cardinal meaning, that buddha making has nothing to do with zazen [insofar as we try to relate them to one another in the ordinary manners of thinking], is unequivocal.[12]

At this point, we should recall what we have previously observed in section 2, namely, the collapse of all hierarchical, teleological, causal, and metaphysical relationships that are assumed to exist between practice and enlightenment. In the present context, it is clear that no amount of tile polishing will ever produce a mirror, insofar as the tile and mirror are two self-sufficient entities or metaphysical opposites and, therefore, are connected in an epistemological, ontological, or other theoretical way. Such stratagems are bound to fail because they do not do full justice to the fundamentally soteriological nature of the matter at hand. That said, let me proceed to the main point: Tile and mirror, or zazen and buddha making (*sabutsu*) can be best understood in terms of soteric foci and as hermeneutic tools, which are less to overcome philosophical impediments—say, by way of a leap of intuition beyond the ken of reason—than to orient and catalyze practitioners' salvific realization. Dōgen is fond of using, in a typically Zen-like fashion, such figurative expressions as "leaping out" (*chōshutsu*) and "leaping into" (*chōnyū*). That which leaps out and/or leaps into is the body-mind, one's whole being.[13] In this context, the whole being is not transported spatially or temporally. Whether leaping out or leaping into, it takes place *reflexively*, as the activities of one-and-the-same reality, also called the dharma world (*hokkai*). If I may adopt the phenomenologist Joachim Wach's definition of religion, Zen's verificational process of realization can be said to be "a total being's total response to a total reality." Dōgen's Zen, however, is thoroughly couched in his nontheist assumption, "One who falls because of the ground rises always because of the very ground" (*chi ni yorite taoruru mono wa kanarazu chi ni yorite oku*). Thus, the tile does not await the mirror, nor does the mirror face the tile. Instead, as the two perspectival foci of zazen's realizational process, they inform and transform each other. The same holds true of the relationship between the self and buddha. All in all, while the tile *is* the mirror, the self *is* buddha in zazen; this undefiledness occurs always at the confluence of tile *and* mirror, of self *and* buddha. It is an event, not a state.

We are now in a position to fully appreciate Dōgen's analysis:

> Chiang-si said, "I strive to make a buddha."
>
> You should thoroughly understand the meaning of this expression. What does it mean to "make a buddha"? Does it mean you are made a buddha by the Buddha? Does it mean to make a buddha of the Buddha? Does it mean the appearance of one or two faces of the Buddha? Does "striving to make a buddha" mean casting off [the body-mind], so that you strive to make a buddha as this casting off? Does "striving to make a buddha" mean that even though "making a buddha" has countless ways, they all continue to be entwined with this "striving"?
>
> Know this: Ta-chi's [Chiang-si Ma-tsu's] words mean that zazen is always "striving to make a buddha," and that zazen is invariably that "striving" which is itself "making a buddha." There is "striving" before "making a buddha"; there is "striving" after "making a buddha"; and there is "striving" right at the moment of "making a buddha." Now let me ask this question: How many [ways of] "buddha making" does such singular "striving" entwine? These entwinings are bound to entwine more entwinings. At this time, entwinings, as the individuated forms of all buddha makings, are always the direct expressions of all the buddha makings, and constitute the individuated forms of striving without exception. You should not shirk this singular striving. When you shirk this singular striving, you will lose your life; even if you lose your life, that in itself is your singular striving's entwining![14]

The crucial importance of the above passage is that Dōgen's soteriological move not only insisted on the nondual unity of the two (meditation and wisdom), but went far beyond it by explicating their dialectical dynamics, namely, by negotiating the Way. In doing so, he parted with some *hongaku* proponents of Kamakura Buddhism, with those members of the Nihon Daruma Sect of Dainichibō Nōnin (n.d.) who tended to be antinomian and fideist, and with those extreme Zen subitists who repudiated meditation in favor of wisdom.

In the above passage, the word *zu* (its verb form being *zu su*), which I translated as "striving," has a wide range of meanings: (1) "to intend," "to desire," "to seek," "to expect," "to look for," and (2) "to plan," "to design," "to organize," "to project," "to picture." The first group of meanings have to do with more or less motivational, aspirational, and intentional workings of the mind, whereas the second with deliberative, rational, and evaluative ones. Roughly speaking, the first category covers the affective and conative functions while the second, the cognitive ones. In Dōgen's conception of the body-mind (*shinjin*), there is no hard-and-fast line drawn in these mental functions, and that is why I have translated *zu* as "striving" in its broadest sense, to involve all forms of aspirations, endeavors, and activities—that is, the whole body-mind.

Dōgen underscores this by saying "zazen is always 'striving to make a buddha' (*zu sabutsu*)," and "zazen is invariably that 'striving' which is *itself* 'making a buddha,'" without facing and awaiting a buddha. As we now know, Dōgen demolished, once and for all, any goal-oriented view of zazen. And yet, he now introduces "striving" in the discussion of zazen. The reason for this is to shift our attention from the aspect of "the unitive awareness" to the aspect of "the revaluated world." As such, striving is making a buddha/being a buddha, as well as casting off/being cast off (*datsuraku*). In fact, striving constitutes the entirety of buddha-realization.

Significantly enough, Dōgen invokes his favorite image of *kattō* ("entwined vines") in his analysis of striving. *Kattō* in Zen parlance signifies the linguistic and conceptual entanglements that become spiritual bondage. However, Dōgen employs the word with positive significations.[15] In the preceding passage, individuated strivings, each singular in their unique way, form a cosmic nexus of entwinings that "are bound to entwine more entwinings." Add to this Dōgen's other notions, such as "the vast and giddy karmic consciousness," "dim-sightedness," and "the nevertheless deluded," and you will see that it is quite fitting for him to highlight the complex and elusive existentiality of the human/cosmic condition, now incorporating human/cosmic strivings that are the vines' omnipresent and intimate entwinings. However tantalizingly elliptic, this is Dōgen's response to Hua-yen's one-in-all and all-in-one. He never privileges striving even at this level of discourse. Instead he calls it "singular striving" (*ichi zu*) to imply one and all simultaneously; that is to say, the singular striving, instead of being metaphysicized, is firmly anchored in existential temporality.

In doing so, Dōgen elucidates dualities—revalorized dualities that, while they are confusions and perplexities in the topsy-turvy world (*zōji tempai*), are now salvific conditions for practitioners to deal with. The underlying logic is clear: Entwined vines must be cut off only by entwined vines themselves; there is no other way.[16] By the same token, dualities are overcome only through dualities themselves. In negotiating the Way, therefore, practitioners cannot escape such fundamental temporal conditions (*jisetsu innen*).

In the preceding, I have endeavored to clarify key aspects of Dōgen's statement quoted at the outset of this chapter: "The endeavor to negotiate the Way, as I teach now, consists in discerning all things in light of enlightenment and putting such a unitive awareness into practice in the midst of the revaluated world." My analysis will also hopefully shed light on what is involved in practitioners' everyday lives, in which they are "thoroughly immersed in mud and water" (*dadei taisui*).[17] At any rate, strivings, entwinings, and dualities are soteriologically legitimized—never abandoned or minimized—as part and parcel of negotiating the Way in the quest for authentic practice.

4

At this juncture, let me briefly touch on the notion of skillful means (*zengyō hōben*; *hōben*) in connection with Dōgen's Zen. Skillful means signifies the buddhas' and celestial bodhisattvas' compassionate means, expedients, and stratagems used to liberate sentient beings—by analogy, the teacher's pedagogical methods to guide his/her students. At the same time, the notion also includes those methods and practices employed by sentient beings (and aspiring bodhisattvas) to attain spiritual realization. This twofold meaning of skillful means—one is the buddhas'/celestial bodhisattvas' accommodative move for the liberation of sentient beings, and the other is sentient beings'/aspiring bodhisattvas' aspirational move toward their salvific goal—developed hand-in-hand early on in the history of the Mahāyāna in various sūtras and śāstras. The culmination of the bodhisattva-way combines the twofold meaning as "seeking enlightenment above, saving sentient beings below" (*jōgu-bodai geke-shujō*), which indicates that skillful means involve benefiting oneself (*jiri*) and benefiting others (*rita*), thereby overcoming the dichotomy of self and other, ascent and descent.

The doctrine's pedagogical and religious values are enormously potent and influential as we examine its role in the history of Buddhism.[18]

Because Dōgen particularly revered the *Lotus Sūtra* as the sūtra of the sūtras, and because one of the most prominent notions propounded in it is none other than the doctrine of skillful means, it is small wonder that he gave considerable appreciation to this doctrine. He highly encouraged the application of skillful means by bringing benefits to all beings through compassionate thoughts and actions.[19] This, however, should be properly understood in view of Dōgen's critical assessment of the doctrine in the context of the unity of practice and enlightenment.

Perhaps the doctrine's most disconcerting aspect, from Dōgen's perspective, is that it treats any skillful action, speech, and thought as a temporary expedient for a higher end (be it wisdom, *nirvāṇa*, buddhahood, or ultimate truth), in accordance with a teleological and hierarchical way of thinking. However skillfully executed and however virtuous, the significance of a means is invariably preliminary and provisional—not ultimate in and of itself. At worst, it may even be false or immoral, as in some duplicitous, opportunistic, and cynical cases, the most infamous of which is the justification of "compassionate killings" (*hōben sesshō*) in a "the-end-justifies-the-means" fashion that appeared in some Buddhist texts. If we push the notion of provisionality to its logical extremity, particularly in the nihilistic interpretation of emptiness, all Buddhist religio-philosophical constructs, myths, symbols, and rituals lose their ultimate validity.[20]

Dōgen seems to have been quite justifiably concerned about some such dangers. If Buddhists' daily activities were nothing more than mere expedients for attaining such goals as the extinction of language (*gongo dōdan*) and the cessation of mental functions (*shingyō shometsu*), worldly affairs, such as government, industry, and commerce, would certainly crumble.[21] The crux of the matter is this: On the one hand, the doctrine has the legitimate function in Buddhist soteriology of encouraging wholesome, compassionate, and efficacious actions, speech, and thoughts on the part of Buddhists; on the other, it has deeply unsettling implications, as noted above. In the face of such dilemmas, Dōgen declares, "'The teaching of skillful means' is itself the unsurpassed workings of the buddha-fruition. The scripture says, 'The Dharma abides in the dharma-situation; worldly affairs always abide [in the Dharma].'" The teaching of skillful means has less to do with provisional expedients than it does with practice and study in and through the entire world of the ten directions.[22] Once again, readers should recall our previous discussion of the collapse of all conventional models regarding the relationship between practice and enlightenment. Similarly, the means and the end should be treated as a pair of foci in Dōgen's Zen. This was in fact Dōgen's forceful response to the *Lotus Sūtra*.

Thus, the *means*, hitherto merely instrumental and provisional, is now thoroughly revalorized as the very core of the end. But note this is neither an absolutization of the means nor a relativization of the end. The traditional dualism of the means and the end is recast as a pair of foci in place of opposites. Rooted in the temporal existentiality of the ongoing realizational process, they catalyze the process, in consistency with the principles of the end, namely wisdom and compassion.

Skillfulness, which traditionally connotes skillfulness in action, speech, and thought, also constitutes practice. To Dōgen's credit, however, he expands the notion: (1) As we shall see later, skillfulness is regarded as indispensable to linguistic sensibility, thinking and reason, and creative imagination, in the soteric milieu, and (2) at the same time, skillfulness is deeply conditioned by humans' dim-sightedness, vast and giddy karmic consciousness, ambiguity, and elusiveness. As seen in this manner, skillful means—now free of the traditional accommodative and aspirational frameworks that smack of the dualistic flaw—becomes the pivot of authentic practice. Dōgen freshens old bottles with new wine.

Parenthetically speaking, the foregoing analysis explains why Dōgen was so highly critical of such Mahāyāna doctrines as the classification of Buddhist teachings (*kyōsō hanjaku*; *kyōhan*), and the three ages of the true dharma, the imitative dharma, and the degenerate dharma (*shō-zō-matsu no sanji*). He was especially critical of the last as the grounds for the necessity of accommodating the Dharma to the intellectual and religious capacities and needs of the audience (*taiki seppō*). Dōgen also criticized the threefold buddha-body (*san-shin*)—the dharma-body, the enjoyment-body, and the transformation-body, as well as Zen's "the finger pointing to the moon" (*shigetsu*). All these notions drew, in one way or another, upon the conventional view of skillful means.

5

Nonduality (*funi*), as the core of the middle way (*chūdō*), is designed to overcome the limitations, restrictions, and dangers inherent in all dualities such as being and nonbeing, defilement and purity, good and evil, knowledge and ignorance, and life and death. Its purpose is to free Buddhist practitioners from clinging to and fixating on those dualities, in order to realize the state of nonduality. As famously presented in the *Vimalakīrti-nirdeśa sūtra*, Vimalakīrti challenges the thirty-two visiting bodhisattvas, including Mañjuśri, to explain how the bodhisattva enters the dharma-gate of nonduality.[23] They each offer their explanations of nonduality and, as a whole, retain the residues of dualism to overcome. Mañjuśri in turn attempts to surmount dualistic elements lurking in his fellow bodhisattvas' interpretations and says: "To know no one teaching, to express nothing, to say nothing, to explain nothing, to announce nothing, to indicate nothing, and to designate nothing—that is the entrance into nonduality." When Mañjuśri asks Vimalakīrti to further elucidate, he "[keeps] his silence, saying nothing at all."[24] In subsequent generations, Zen Buddhists have been fond of calling Vimalakīrti's silence as "a singular, thunderous silence" (*ichimoku rai no gotoshi*) that transcends the duality of speech and silence.

Dōgen's assessment of Vimalakīrti's silence is, not surprisingly, uncharitable:

> They [Zen teachers of T'ang and Sung China] say: "Vimalakīrti demonstrated the truth to the bodhisattvas by keeping his silence and saying nothing at all. That is the same as the Tathāgata's saying nothing at all in order to enlighten others." Such a view indicates an utter ignorance of the Buddha-dharma and the lack of any capacity to study the Way. The Tathāgata's speech is clearly different from that of all others; likewise, regarding silence, he and other beings are not the same. For this reason, the Tathāgata's silence and Vimalakīrti's silence—you cannot even compare their similarities. . . . As I observe Sung China today, the people who have studied the great Way of the buddha-ancestors seem to be extinct. Not even two or three people can be found. There are only those who believe that while Vimalakīrti was superior in keeping his singular silence, the latter-day people who lack such a silence are inferior to him. No field of the Buddha-dharma's activities is thus left any more.[25]

However "thunderous" Vimalakīrti's silence may be, and however nondual his nonduality may be in transcending the duality of speech and silence, Dōgen is emphatic in pointing out fundamental flaws in not only his but also traditional Zen's conception of nonduality. These flaws encourage complacency in silence and fail to address nonduality's dynamicity in relation to duality—namely, speech. Nonduality is not privileged or transcendentalized metaphysically any more than duality. It is simply one of the soteric foci within the process of realization. This observation will be fully explored later in the present work. It should be noted for now that, in its liberating process, nonduality embraces duality rather than abandons it. Consequently, nonduality is *not* extra-, trans-, pre-, post-, or antiduality. It is always necessarily rooted in duality. Therefore, *non*duality

functions within, with, and through *duality*. The non in nonduality signifies dynamicity.

Surprisingly, this pivotal premise has been often overlooked, ignored,
or forgotten. Yet it merits our utmost attention, especially in Dōgen's Zen.
The dynamic dialectics involved in the process is traditionally characterized as "not two and not one" *(funi fuichi)*, or "neither the one nor the many"
(fuichi fui). Duality and nonduality are incumbent on each other. Furthermore, they interpenetrate in the manner that "as one side is illumined, the
other is darkened." Both duality and nonduality in the Buddhist tradition
are governed by emptiness, a notion that radically rejects the substantiality
of any beings—persons and things alike.

At this juncture, let me dwell briefly on the notion of foci that I
have so far only passingly noted. I now suggest that, insofar as understanding Dōgen is concerned, the binary notions of the so-called opposites,
antitheses, and polarities are best construed as foci after their scrutiny and
revaluation. My reason is this: Religious thinkers and philosophers, in the
East and West alike, have generally employed those opposites ontologically
and epistemologically within various metaphysical (substantialist) worldviews, thus implying the dualistic way of thinking. The problem with the
logical, teleological, central-peripheral frameworks has already been noted
earlier in this chapter. Zen's traditional critique of dualism as couched in
discrimination *(funbetsu)* has been leveled almost exclusively at dualistic
implications and the dangers inherent in those substantialist worldviews.
The other side of the coin, however, is that it has failed to critically address
the *possibility of duality* free of dualism and the enormous malleability and
versatility of language, and that it has overzealously attempted to eliminate, rather than reform, dualisms.

As a well-known Zen adage illustrates, a finger certainly can point
to the moon, but it can also do many other things in a number of different
situations. Even "dividing reality" (the literal meaning of *funbetsu*) can be
done for many different purposes and with many different intentions. My
adoption of "foci" as soteriological, perspectival, and pragmatic (though I
would use this word sparingly in Dōgen's context) purports to (1) explicate the dialectical dynamics of duality and nonduality clear of substantialist, representational, and dualistic implications, and (2) underline the
dynamic, multidimensional functions of duality—that is, discriminative
thinking as well as language. Thus, the paramount functions of all salvific
foci, including duality and nonduality, consist of orienting, guiding, fa-
cilitating, catalyzing, empowering, informing, transforming, and purify-
ing practitioners' ongoing realizational processes. As such, they are *living*

and lived forces within the dynamics of realization. Duality and nonduality and their relationship in the paradoxical juxtaposition of not-twoness and not-oneness are principles that govern all pairs of foci in Dōgen's Zen. In this respect, duality and nonduality might well be called the *root foci*. Most importantly, all the foci are thoroughly embedded in the temporality of existence-time (*uji*).

Having said this, two further observations on the issue of duality and nonduality, often expressed in terms of differentiation (*shabetsu*) and equality (*byōdō*), are in order. First, nonduality is all too often misunderstood as neutrality, indifference, undifferentiation, atemporality, freedom from moral choice and commitment, and so forth. It should be remembered, however, that "a unitive awareness" (of nonduality), which I previously rendered for *ichinyo* at the beginning of the present chapter, is still elliptic at best because, however transcendent, total, and veridical, it is in essence a valuational notion of a specific worldview. As such, it should not usurp the claim of universality over other worldviews and religions in the pluralist world. To do so would be hubristic and overzealous regarding what it is and does. This point can hardly be overemphasized in view of the central thrust of temporality in Dōgen's praxis-oriented religion.

On the other hand, often unjustifiably welded into the notion of nonduality has been the most prevalent conception of Zen—largely attributed to D. T. Suzuki—that the essence of Zen consists in the unmediated enlightenment experience (or state of consciousness), totally untainted by ideational and valuational mediations as well as by historical and social conditions. The pure experience (or pure consciousness)—*sui generis*, ineffable and ahistorical—is as such the universal experiential core from which all religions originate and to which they all return. This is the Zen version of *philosophia perennis*, with added Zen and Japanese flavors. Such a Zen, as I see it, is not Dōgen's, because nonduality in this view is thoroughly metaphysicized, rarefied, and disembodied so much so that it is ineffective and ineffectual from the standpoint of authentic practice. Furthermore, the arrogation of unlimited universality to itself is flatly contrary to the logic of temporality—situatedness in a specific time and place as a dharma-situation (*hōi*)—as unmistakably enunciated in Dōgen's Zen.[26]

In this connection, Robert H. Sharf's observations on the rhetoric and ideology of enlightenment experience is extremely instructive for understanding the temporality of nonduality. In his two essays on the subject, Sharf delineates historically and conceptually the modern intellectual construction of Zen by some Zen apologists such as Suzuki in response to the pressing issues of modernity. Particularly noteworthy is Sharf's analysis of the notion of "pure experience" and its role in Suzuki's Zen that in the final analysis amounts to the advocacy of (1) Zen's privileged perspective which transcends all religions and cultures, (2) Zen as the moral, aesthetic, metaphysical, and spiritual ground of Japanese culture itself, and (3) Zen spirituality, at once unique and universal, as affirming the uniqueness and supremacy of Japanese culture.[27] This is cultural/spiritual nationalism—Bernard Faure dubs it "reverse Orientalism" or "Zen Orientalism"[28]—which Suzuki, along with his philosopher friend Nishida Kitarō of the Kyoto School, bequeathed to such modern Japanese intellectuals as Nishitani Keiji, Hisamatsu Shin'ichi, and Abe Masao, to name just a few.[29] Such a cultural/spiritual nationalist sentiment might also be indirectly related to *nihonjinron*, the Japanese uniqueness polemics that emerged in recent decades and continues to this day.[30]

In the context of Dōgen's view of nonduality, Sharf's thesis reminds Zen practitioners of their experience being inevitably enmeshed with religious and institutional factors, as well as historical and social conditions. Thus nonduality is necessarily mediated by duality, just as they are predicated upon one another. As noted before in the preceding chapter, the mystery and paradox of clarity and ambiguity, of emptiness and dimsightedness, and of delusion and enlightenment remain true of the experiential immediacy of nonduality as well. This immediacy in question may be undoubtedly genuine and self-validating, yet in and of itself should not be equated to the absence of mediation.

Second, duality in the context of nonduality as delineated above should be distinguished from dualism with those impediments to soteric realization that originate in the misappropriation of discriminative mental and linguistic acts. Accordingly, it is that old dualism which is re-visioned. For our analysis, this distinction between duality and dualism is crucial. More often than not, Zen Buddhists are prone to construe that duality as such is intrinsically bad, and hence should be surmounted or annihilated, or at best, should be regarded as a necessary evil to endure. This traditionalist view is founded, as noted already, on the restrictive conception of duality and language. As we shall consider further, Dōgen's view on this subject, particularly on language, is a far cry from such a conventional one, although he was all too aware of its fundamental limitations and dangers. At any rate, it is absolutely imperative for practitioners to deal with their everyday lives by continually making choices, decisions, and commitments, in terms of revaluated dualities that are informed and empowered by nonduality. In order to effectively engage in the task of daily affairs, they must employ language, the intellect, and critical thinking as a common basis for dialogue and communication with one another, whether they are Buddhists or non-Buddhists, religionists or secularists. Thus, negotiating the Way in pursuit of authentic practice consists in how to do Zen with nondually revaluated duality, now recast in terms of the various pairs of foci.

Duality, however, is inevitably involved in human frailties, ambiguities, and vulnerabilities. Although human nature is finite and imperfect, it also has the capacity to know, and the desire and obligation to fulfill, whatever possibilities exist at the interface of its fallibility and perfectibility. The bounds of both are ultimately unknown—"bottomlessly elusive" (*mutan*) in Dōgen's words. Tensions and conflicts between the fallibility and perfectibility of human nature thus constitute the substance of all forms of duality. In view of such an assessment of the human condition, it is vitally important for practitioners to realize that, despite such an egregious ideologization of Zen as in Imperial Way Zen (*kōdō zen*),[31] Dōgen's reflections on "A mirror never reflects again; a flower never returns to the tree" quietly remind them of the soteric imperative for critical self-understanding of profound ambiguity that is "ever intimate" with one's allegedly self-validating enlightenment. This is why duality must be continually kept alive in the *verificational* dynamics of practice-enlightenment.

All in all, the dynamic dialectics of duality and nonduality is a thread that runs through Dōgen's religious method on how authentically to do Zen. Throughout his monastic career he endeavored to explore and examine the richness and complexity of the logic of duality in a radically temporal, yet nondual situation. I submit that his undertaking in this regard, however fragmentary and elliptic, remains his lasting contribution to Zen discourse and praxis.

6

By way of concluding this chapter let me make a few additional points:

1. The (nondual) *unity* of practice and enlightenment is not so much a metaphysical or supernatural given beyond the practice-enlightenment dynamics as it is the quality of authenticity that is, on the one hand, "ever already" (*isō*)[32] realized and, on the other, paradoxically constantly perfected by practitioners in the "ever deluded" (*kyakumei*) condition. "Undefiledness" (*fuzenna*) lies in the nature and dynamics of the unity of practice and enlightenment, never in the abolition of duality. This is the kernel of negotiating the Way.

2. Practice is all too often misunderstood in such a way that ethical, rational, and critical thinking are merely preliminary and adventitious to enlightenment—stepping stones at best and detrimental hindrances at worst. As I shall discuss in subsequent chapters, Dōgen's treatment of nondually revalorized duality in its multifarious workings show otherwise. Intellectual endeavor and critical rigor are intrinsic to enlightenment and, hence, are part and parcel of practice.

3. "Seeing things as they are" is a soteriological vision that subverts and renews itself constantly, ad infinitum. Dōgen calls this *tōdatsu* ("liberation"), short for *tōtai datsuraku*, which means "penetrating and casting off the whole being" *and* "the whole being penetrated and cast off." The vision of "things as they are" is never of a fixed reality/truth; the power for self-subversion and self-renewal is inherent in the vision itself. Thus "things" seen as they are are transformable. Every practitioner's task is to *change* them by seeing through them. From Dōgen's perspective, this is the fundamental difference between contemplation (*dhyāna*) and zazen-only. To him, seeing was changing and making.

4. Just like delusion and enlightenment (*meigo*), practice and enlightenment (*shushō*) are beginningless and endless, coterminous and coeternal, and thoroughly temporal, yet not the captive of temporality. Despite these structural similarities, the difference between them should not be overlooked. The difference is that, while regarding delusion and enlightenment, the thrust is humans' intellectual, moral, and existential ambiguity in terms of their primordial opacity or their "dim-sightedness," such an existential humility scarcely appears in the foreground of the discourse on practice and enlightenment, and instead we find vigor and boldness on the part of Dōgen, who exhorts his disciples to assiduously practice, and thereby participate in the buddha-ancestors' salvific enterprise. Yet, remember Dōgen's dictum: "As one side is illumined, the other is darkened." Both aspects complement one another within the dynamics of realization. In this manner, Dōgen offers an important desideratum for Zen practitioners' wholesome praxis.

CHAPTER 3

Weighing Emptiness

I

Dōgen's appropriation of emptiness is characteristically praxis oriented, through and through. This may not be altogether surprising in view of the fact that Zen (Ch'an) is construed as a practically oriented school of Mahāyāna Buddhism, as compared with such ones as Tendai (T'ien-t'ai) and Kegon (Hua-yen) that have often been said to be doctrinally oriented. The question, however, is what sort of practice we are talking about—one that is vulnerable to antinomianism and anti-intellectualism or one that does full justice to all aspects of human life and beyond. The proclivity to privilege equality (byōdō), as often pointed out by scholars in Zen, tends to devalue or erase differentiation (shabetsu), thereby entailing the weakening and, at worst, the disavowal of critical thinking in the ethical, political, and social spheres. As a result, Zen has more often than not been vulnerable to a culture religion or a situation ethic by all too facilely and uncritically acceding to power and the status quo. A case in point, for example, may be cited:

> Zen has no special doctrine or philosophy, no set of concepts or intellectual formulas except that it tries to release one from the bondage of birth and death, by means of certain intuitive modes of understanding peculiar to itself. It is, therefore, extremely flexible in adapting itself to almost any philosophy and moral doctrine as long as its intuitive teaching is not interfered with. It may be found wedded to anarchism or fascism, communism or democracy, atheism or idealism, or any political or economic dogmatism.[1]

Is this the way you "see things as they are"? I do not wish to dwell on an analysis of the above statement in this chapter. Suffice it to say that such an excessive adaptability or flexibility of Zen to a given situation is due, at least in part, to its flawed view of the soteriological significance of emptiness.

As seen against this backdrop, however, nowhere is this issue more clearly challenged than in Dōgen's exposition of dream (*yume*; *mu*) in the *Shōbōgenzō*, "Muchū setsumu" fascicle (1242), where he touches on the crux of the matter in an extremely elliptic and suggestive, yet illuminating, manner.

2

The notion of dream is variously dealt with in Buddhism; its usages and functions are multiple. It is noteworthy that dream in the Buddhist tradition in general occurs only to beings in the realm of desires, one of the triple world (the other two are the realms of form and formlessness); free of desires and wishes, the buddhas are regarded as having no dreams. The word *dream* connotes the evanescent and short-lived nature of life and reality as in "dreams and phantoms, bubbles and shadows" (*mugen bōyō*), and is also employed as a metaphor for the nonsubstantiality and emptiness of things. Although it plays an important role in folk Buddhism in communicating with the gods and spirits, understanding the past and present, and foretelling the future, dream is by and large marginalized in official Buddhist discourse as representing the illusory and irrational in contradistinction to the real and rational. Dualism between the dream state and the waking state, between reality and illusion, is the undercurrent here.

Characteristics of Dōgen's treatment of dream in the "Muchū setsumu" fascicle are threefold: First, he reclaimed the notion of dream from its neglect and obscurity. As I have discussed in some detail elsewhere,[2] Dōgen often resuscitates those symbols and notions hitherto forgotten, slighted, or abandoned, thereby rediscovering or reconstructing surprisingly novel, insightful meanings for them. The fascicle was presented in 1242 in Kyoto, just prior to his relocation to Echizen (present-day Fukui prefecture) in 1243; Dōgen was at the height of intellectual creativity during this period. The "Zazenshin" fascicle, which was discussed before and will be considered again later, was written earlier in the same year and took up another denigrated notion of thinking in relation to meditation. The two fascicles offer a religious method that radicalizes the understanding and practicing of Zen. In them, Dōgen brings the peripheral, obscure, ambiguous, and dubious in everyday experience to the center of our awareness by giving them fundamental salvific significance. Zen soteriology excludes nothing from its purview; not only that, it declares dream as "central" by overturning our habitual dualism of the center and periphery.

Second, Dōgen overcomes the bifurcation of dream and waking, and says:

> In the waking state, there are arousing the mind, training, enlightenment, and *nirvāṇa*; in the dream state, there are arousing the mind, training, enlightenment, and *nirvāṇa*. The dream state and the waking state are equally ultimate reality. They have nothing whatsoever to do with largeness and smallness, or superiority and inferiority.[3]

Dualisms between dream and waking, reality and illusion, and the rational and irrational are now thoroughly dismantled and reconstituted in Zen discourse as (revaluated) dualities that intertwine and interpenetrate one another. Furthermore, "dream and awakening are originally one."[4] The identity of dream and awakening, as we have observed in chapter 1 in connection with dim-sightedness, shows that the more penetrating our understanding of dream, the deeper our realization of awakening. Dream expands the scope, depth, and precision of awakening.

Third, Dōgen's religious method firmly grounds itself in the conditions of existence—temporality. He boldly contends that all is dream, and nothing but dream. Yet that is not all he has to say:

> Every crystal-clear manifestation of the entire world is a dream; this dream is none other than all things that are absolutely lucid. One's doubt of this itself is a dream; life's confusion is a dream as well. At this very moment, all things are a dream, are within a dream, and expound a dream. As we study things, roots and stalks, branches and leaves, flowers and fruits, lights and colors—all are a great dream. Never mistake this for a dreamy state of mind.
>
> Such being the case, those who shun the study of the Buddha-way while encountering the expounding of a dream within a dream, absurdly think that people misconstrue the things of dreams as real and consequently pile up delusion on top of delusion. This is not true. Even though it is said, "One is further deluded *amid* delusion," you should correctly construe it as saying, "One is further deluded *beyond* delusion." In such an understanding lies the path of progress in realization.[5]

Note that "One is further deluded *amid* delusion" is now rendered as "One is further deluded *beyond* delusion." Substitute "dream" for "delusion," and we can understand the gist of these statements properly in our present hermeneutic context, for the same logic applies to delusion and dream alike.[6] Both "*amid* delusion/dream" and "*beyond* delusion/dream" take place in the human condition. The former addresses human fallibility whereas the latter human perfectibility; both possibilities are dialectically related to one another, dually and nondually. What should be noted for our purpose in this chapter is that the differences between fallibility and perfectibility are never blunted in Dōgen's Zen. Thus, "the path of progress in realization" consists not in supplanting dream so much as clarifying, penetrating, and surpassing it in and through itself.

From this perspective, Dōgen considers *muchū setsumu,* "*expounding* a dream within a dream," as *musa muchū,* "dream *making* within a dream." A dream in his view is not merely a necessary illusion or a necessary fiction that brings about a soteriological reality/truth; this would smack of dualism by implying a nonfictional or nonillusory reality that remains yet to be realized. Rather, Dōgen suggests that inasmuch as there is no way out of the dream, the only "way out" available to practitioners—which is itself a dream—is to live within a dream, to go beyond a dream by way of expounding/making a dream. As we shall see presently, Dōgen's commentary is closely interwoven with the notion of emptiness, especially with what I would call the reconstructive aspect of the notion—in contrast to the deconstructive one.

3

In the course of his exposition on dream in "Muchū setsumu," Dōgen suddenly introduces the analogy of a steelyard. This key passage describes the dynamic workings of emptiness via the image of a dream:

> Study a steelyard in equilibrium. When we study it, our power to discern minute differences in weight manifests itself without fail, and thus puts forth the expounding of a dream within a dream. Unless we consider weight differences, and thereby attain the equilibrium [of the steelyard], no fairness [in the ascertainment of weight] is accomplished. Only when equilibrium is obtained, do we see fairness. Once we have obtained equilibrium, it does not hinge upon the object [to be weighed], the steelyard, or its workings. You must investigate the following thoroughly: Although [the object, the steelyard, and its workings] hang in empty space, if you do not bring about equilibrium, fairness is not materialized. Just as [the steelyard] itself hangs in emptiness, so does it accept things [to be weighed, regardless of their weight] and lets them play freely in emptiness. Such is the expounding of a dream within a dream. In emptiness [the steelyard] embodies equilibrium; fairness is the great principle of the steelyard. [By virtue of this principle of fairness] we weigh emptiness and things; whether it be emptiness or form, [we weigh it to] meet fairness. This is the expounding of a dream within a

dream as well. In no case is there liberation that does not expound a dream within a dream. A dream is the entire great earth; the entire great earth is in equilibrium. For this reason, the vertiginous confusions of life are limitless; this is the attestation of a dream within dream. We welcome them in faith and live them in reverence.[7]

In the fascicle, the above passage stands out with its unequivocal thrust, and yet, commentarial works in the Sōtō tradition have conveniently muted and trivialized its true significance to the extent that they have virtually buried it, instead favoring the static, uncritical, transcendentalistic meaning of emptiness in the name of equality. Nevertheless, despite its extreme brevity, the passage has fundamental importance for what I propose to discuss in the present chapter: Emptiness cares about differences in worldly truth so as to bring about fairness.

In the olden days, people used a steelyard, or a portable unequal-arm balance, to measure the weight of an object. The beam of a steelyard consists of two unequal portions: The shorter one has a hook or pan for holding the object to be weighed and the longer one has a scale and movable counterpoise for obtaining the weight of the object. The steelyard is suspended at the point where these two portions, or arms, of the beam meet. One determines the accurate weight of the object by moving the counterpoise along the scale of the longer arm in order to attain equilibrium of the object and the counterpoise. When in disequilibrium, the beam moves in a seesaw manner; when in equilibrium, it is completely still. In this way, an object's unknown weight can be found through the counterpoise's known weight. In a broader context, then, the beam with unequal arms, the object to be weighed, the counterpoise moving along the scale, the person who weighs, the force of gravity operative in the physics of the steelyard, and the rest—all work delicately in concert with one another, in accordance with dependent origination to attain equilibrium, fairness, and reasonableness in commercial transactions.

The original word *kū* for "the sky," "space," and "the air," also means "emptiness" (*śūnyatā*), a pivotal Mahāyāna Buddhist concept, and Dōgen adroitly makes use of *kū*'s multiple meanings so as to elicit an evocative and profound image of what is involved in our subject matter at hand. His expression *kū ni kakareri* means at once "hanging in empty space" and "hanging in emptiness." Elsewhere, Dōgen uses *kokū ni kakaru/ka kokū* and *kokū ni kakareri* for "hanging in empty space."[8] "Hanging" in the present case draws on the fact that the steelyard, when in use, is suspended from the hand of one who weighs. By extension, the object to be weighed, the person who weighs, the steelyard, and its functioning are all suspended in the air, in emptiness.

In this light, I suggest readers to imagine a person who is being suspended in a vast expanse of empty space that holds nothing whatsoever in any direction. However far one may look, there is nothing to secure a foothold or handhold on, just empty space itself. Empty space has no foundation, no substratum, and no boundary; it is absolutely void and boundlessly open.[9] This analogy, obviously derived from that of "hanging in empty space," has radically subversive overtones. The situation of being left high up in midair is indeed terrifying and maddening existentially, for knowing that things, ideas, and values have no self-nature and that there is nothing whatsoever to cling to is an unbearable threat to our whole way of life. It deconstructs our conventional worldviews so relentlessly that nothing is left to rely on and feel certain of. And yet, this is precisely what practitioners must grapple with—a complete collapse of the reificational way of thinking and its implications. Only then can they realize a truly liberating, responsible religiosity.

A few caveats regarding this should be mentioned. The words *empty space* may suggest a receptacle (or an absolute space) in which all things are contained, but this is not so. Dōgen says: "When the sky flies off, the bird flies off; when the bird flies off, the sky flies off. Speaking of the investigation of this flying off, we say: 'It is just here!'"[10] Time does not move in space; time *is* space, hence time and space *move* together. In other words, space is not only not atemporalized but dynamic—it is movable.[11] Nor is empty space that source or origin to which the ten thousand things return, as in Lao-tzu's familiar image.[12] Dōgen emphatically rejects the widely held view of meditation in Zen as "returning to the source, back to the origin" (*gengen hempon*).[13] For these reasons Dōgen writes: "The whole body of empty space hangs in empty space."[14] Just as space is radically temporalized, so is emptiness in Dōgen's Zen.

Dōgen once fondly recalled his deceased master Ju-ching's poem:

> The whole body [of a wind-bell] is like the mouth
>   hanging in empty space.
> Regardless of which direction the wind blows from—
>   East, West, South, or North,
> Steadfastly it speaks of wisdom for others.
>   Tinkle! Tinkle! Tinkle![15]

Poeticizing emptiness, Ju-ching read the whole body of a wind-bell/the mouth as hanging in empty space while tinkling the sound of wisdom.

Similarly, on the same subject, Dōgen renders the steelyard and things to be weighed as both hanging in empty space while playing freely and engaging in transformative activities (*yuke*). Both Ju-ching and Dōgen here are thoroughly attuned to the *embodied* emptiness in its totality. "*The whole body* of empty space hangs in empty space," as quoted above, may appear very similar in philosophical tenor to, for instance, Mādhyamika philosophy's "the emptiness of emptiness" (*śūnyatā śūnyatā*);[16] yet, "the whole body" concretizes empty space/emptiness in a typically Zen Buddhist fashion so that, following Dōgen's favorite idioms, the whole body is "totally exerted" (*gūjin*) and "cast off" (*datsuraku*) simultaneously.

The point I wish to underscore is that Dōgen's appropriation of emptiness is not just confined to a deconstructive function that demolishes every possible reificational and representational delusion, but engaged in a reconstructive function in the temporality of the whole body with its salvific efficacy—not only experientially but also conceptually and linguistically. Emptiness enables practitioners to discern that the existential and spiritual predicament of hanging in empty space, however abysmal, frightening, and uncertain, is none other than the liberating occasion of "right this moment" (*shōtō immoji*), with an inclusive sense of efficacy. It works internally so as to cleanse practitioners of all essentialist traces and props and to catalyze physical and mental forces for the acquirement of realization. As we shall see more clearly later, Dōgen's deconstructive stance is as thorough and relentless as possible; even so, in Dōgen's praxis orientation, his appropriation of emptiness is preeminently reconstructive—ethical, linguistic, and rational.

4

We are now in a position to examine the pivotally important aspect of our investigation, namely, Dōgen's reconstructive way of thinking regarding emptiness. In speaking of "hanging/playing freely in empty space," Dōgen provides an intriguing principle to consider by referring to "the equilibrium of the steelyard." As usual, he plays with the semantic possibilities of the word *hei* which means "even," "impartial," "equal," "ordinary," "common," "peaceful," "harmonious," and significantly enough for our present subject matter, "to regulate" and "to weigh." In particular, he adopts the two cardinal significations of *hei*: *Equilibrium* as essential for the physical operation of the steelyard and *fairness* as "the great principle" of this instrument. Understanding the subtle blending of equilibrium and fairness in his usage of *hei* is the core of the steelyard analogy.

Fairness now alludes to equality (*byōdō*) in Buddhist philosophy. As seen previously, equality is all too often privileged over differentiation (*shabetsu*)—despite their nonduality (*byōdō soku shabetsu*)—so much so that differentiation is rendered as all but ineffectual, and even drastically neutralized at worst. This has been the congenital disease in Mahāyāna in general and Zen in particular. In view of this, it is a pleasant surprise to discover Dōgen's brief excursion, however passing, to the analogy of effecting the equilibrium of the steelyard by measuring calibrations on the beam, with its enormous implications for understanding and practicing Zen. This excursion takes place in the context of his discourse on dream, empty space, and emptiness. The analogy of weighing or measuring weight (*kakeru*) is key here. "Unless we consider weight differences, and thereby attain the equilibrium [of the steelyard], no fairness [in the ascertainment of weight] is accomplished. Only when equilibrium is obtained, do we see fairness," writes Dōgen. "Although [the object, the steelyard, and its workings] hang in empty space, if you do not bring about equilibrium, fairness is not materialized." In other words, equilibrium is not a given, but attained by virtue of weighing and negotiating (weight) differences. Careful calibrating activity through discerning and discriminative eyes is the sine qua non of fairness. Accordingly, emptiness involves the dynamics of weighing and calibration on the one hand and the principle of fairness and reasonableness on the other.

When the steelyard is in equilibrium, it is at rest, with no more swings of the beam to one side or the other. The static appearance of the steelyard at rest belies the dynamic process of weighing/fairness; precise measuring is a requisite for accuracy in weight reading and fair dealings. By the same token, emptiness may appear static, abstract, or one-dimensional, and yet in reality, particularly in relation to dependent origination and worldly truth (i.e., in the two truths), it is dynamic, concrete, and multi-dimensional in its workings. As a result, discriminative discernment regarding differentiation (duality) in our everyday life is intrinsic, not extrinsic, to equality (nonduality). Equality does not exist or subsist in the abstract, independent of such a dynamic negotiation of differentiation, any more than fairness exists apart from the process of equilibration. In dealing with the nondual unity of equality and differentiation, Dōgen now explicates the dynamic dialectics between these two foci in terms of the activities of weighing/measuring (equilibration) and the principle of fairness (equilibrium). Just as enlightenment is to practice, so is fairness to equilibration. Dōgen's Zen, as I see it, may be said to be an amplification of this fundamental theme.

Thus in the mundane situation, the balancing efforts of weighing, measuring, and calibrating (and by extension, reasoning, reflection, and deliberation) must go on incessantly—consciously and unconsciously, intrapersonally and interpersonally, locally and globally, and beyond—in order to generate fairness as the conditions of that situation change. (We should recall our previous discussion of skillful means. Skillfulness and compassion are now addressed by way of weighing facts, values, conditions, contexts, and whatnot.) Dōgen construes such a process of equilibration as "expounding a dream," whereas the state of equilibrium as "within a dream."

In light of this analysis, his statement, "Once we have obtained equilibrium, it does not hinge upon the object [to be weighed], the steelyard, or its workings," should be properly understood. Dōgen here reminds us of the realizational context of equilibration and equilibrium. Upon the breakdown of the logical, causal, teleological, and other relationships of various metaphysical opposites, Dōgen would envision the relationship between equilibration and equilibrium by way of such metaphors and analogies as "intimacy," "entwined vines," "as one side is illumined, the other is darkened," and so forth. In this respect, they are better conceived as a pair of two foci in the dynamics of realization, neither of which is facilely reduced to or privileged over the other. The discontinuity between these foci is never overstated as incommensurable. In other words, Dōgen locates the continuity and discontinuity between equilibration and equilibrium (and I might add, between the worldly truth and ultimate truth of Mādhyamika thought) within the temporal process of realization in order to conduce to authentic practice.

It is also noteworthy that while Dōgen vehemently opposes understanding the Buddha-dharma strictly in terms of human standards and measures in a reductive fashion, he nonetheless heavily draws upon those notions associated with quantity and number.[17] For example, the word *ryō* (originally, the Sino-Buddhist translation of Sanskrit *pramāṇa*, "the means of valid cognition or knowledge") is employed in many different ways, as in *ninryō* and *jōryō* (both meaning "human comprehension"), *butsuryō* ("buddha-measure," "buddha-knowledge"), *hōryō* ("dharma-measure," "dharma-knowledge"), and *goryō* ("enlightenment-measure," "enlightenment-knowledge"). The *ryō* is also cognate to such verbs as *hakaru/ryōsu* ("to measure," "to deliberate," "to calculate"), *shikiryōsu* ("to survey," "to estimate"), and as noted before, *kakeru* ("to weigh"). These examples are indicative of Dōgen's sensitivity to and respect for quantity and number—those denigrated attributes of the physical world and the activities associated with them, such as measurement, comparison, and evaluation. Yet

such quantitative attributes and activities are now soteriological impera-
tives in Dōgen's Zen precisely because of their fundamental importance in
determining fairness, impartiality, skillfulness, and reasonableness. Dōgen
subsumes these principles and virtues under the term *dōri* or "reason," as I
shall further discuss in another chapter.

5

Soteric reality/truth in Dōgen's Zen might be clarified in terms of the
nonrational, elusive, and indeterminate on the one hand, and the rational,
obvious, and determinate on the other. In dynamic dialectics, all dreams
are so intertwined and interpenetrated with one another that the boundary between the two is altogether fragile and ephemeral. Along with this
picture of the entwinement of the rational and nonrational as in the image
of "entwined vines," it is to be noted that the nonrational is not necessarily
irrational, and the rational is not always rational; both are vulnerable to irrationality and unreason. More importantly, the irrational in Dōgen's Zen
are also dreams, for the logic of emptiness demands the inclusion of the
irrational in its domain. In light of his re-visioned web of the nonrational,
rational, and irrational such as this, reality/truth is thoroughly temporal,
being stripped of its time-honored privilege, presumption, and hubris.
Expounding a dream within a dream as a salvific process of realization is
construed in the broadest possible context.

That said, the significance of the weighing analogy becomes apparent. Neither an absolutist nor a nihilist, and instead a staunch "temporal-
ist" if you will, Dōgen calls for the necessity of practitioners to critically
understand, evaluate, and construct their beliefs and values, principles and
virtues. A critical, constructive negotiation between weighing and fairness
involves an enormous range of activities that are comprised of methods,
strategies, and analyses in countless fashions in response to the challenges
of an ever-changing situation.[18] In this respect, weighing may seem to con-
verge with the doctrine of skillful means, and yet, it focuses more acutely
than the latter on the role of critical, rational, and moral reflections and
deliberations for the execution of practice and enlightenment in the midst
of life's situation. It goes without saying that Dōgen would never situate
weighing in the teleological means-end scheme, nor in the-end-justifies-
the-means model. As noted before, he is clearly aware of the inherent sus-
ceptibility of the doctrine to such misuses and abuses. Remember at this
point that the dynamics of emptiness (preeminently present in the weighing act) can never be vacuous, neutral, or value free, in order to permit

practitioners an intellectual and moral holiday. The cultivation of critical acumen is requisite for doing Zen authentically.

Even so, the weighing task in the concrete human situation is extremely difficult for practitioners, due to personal, economic, political, and social conditions, all of which must be carefully taken into consideration so as to determine equitable and just actions and transactions—as, for example, in dealing with the categories traditionally called "the eightfold path" in Buddhism.[19] From the etic perspective, personal motives and reasons, as well as institutional interests and agendas, are microscopically dissected by modern and postmodern thinkers such as the masters of suspicion (Marx, Nietzsche, Freud) and their followers. Thanks to them we are now aware of the beguiling and treacherous textures of not only human nature, but also institutions and ideologies, far more deeply than ever before. The weighing task as criticism may also be applicable to practitioners themselves as self-critique or self-understanding from the emic perspective. Here again, practitioners should be reminded of Dōgen's insight into human nature's "bottomless elusiveness" (*mutan*)—in terms of its capacity for self-deception and self-centeredness. Add fairness and its cognates, such as justice and reasonableness, to this picture and the weighing task becomes more and more complex and complicated. How do we define fairness? Justice? Reasonableness? A pivotal point to note at this moment is that emptiness, as Dōgen sees it, is invariably rooted in the weighing task—all the way from initial deliberation to decision making to the execution of action in each and every area of daily life. Despite the seemingly abstract, airy aura surrounding his discourse on dream, empty space, and emptiness, Dōgen is concerned with the nitty-gritty reality of our flesh-and-blood existence from which we cannot escape for a moment when it comes to the pressing matters of truth and meaning, right and wrong, good and bad, just and unjust, and so forth. Encountering moral and existential dilemmas and perplexities, our "vast and giddy karmic consciousness" must still operate in full capacity to choose, decide, and act, not only for mere survival but for authentic living. This is the situation in which emptiness is "shattered" and "fallen," and which, nevertheless, is supposed to effectively function despite its shattered, fallen state.

In this context, can enlightenment be free of all-too-human dilemmas and contradictions and still claim to be enlightenment? We now know that Dōgen's answer is an emphatic "no." Enlightenment posited in such an existential vacuity, however intellectually and spiritually lofty, is nevertheless an ineffectual, not fully engaged life. Even so, a flight into the realm of equality immunized against differentiation is itself a choice, an action;

equality, as much as differentiation, is no more than a mode of existence-time (*uji*). As such, it is in the final analysis a dream that should be subject to rigorous examination through a finely calibrating, discriminative eye. This is the task of *expounding a dream* (or dream making) within a dream.

"For this reason," writes Dōgen, "the vertiginous confusions of life (*kaitō tennō*) are limitless—this is the attestation of a dream within a dream." The greater practitioners' confusions, the more their endeavors for fairness and justice are called for, pointing to their ever vigorous commitment to critical understanding and analysis. Dōgen lived in medieval Japan, the ethos of which was deeply perplexing and chaotic. Against the backdrop of his age and between the lines of his writings, we can read his anguish and pain, as well as his joy and wonderment, with respect to human existence, the human condition, and beyond—all while boldly and humbly carrying out his salvific project. What practitioners can gain from Dōgen is less a solution or answer than a new direction. Dōgen's view, as sketched above in the steelyard analogy, points to such a new direction in Zen thinking.

6

In order to shed further light on Dōgen's view of emptiness, I wish to return to the subject of the two truths briefly touched on before. I find C. W. Huntington, Jr.'s exposition of Candrakīrti (c.600–650), a Prāsaṅgika proponent of Mādhyamika thought in India, to be very useful in the present context.[20] Huntington holds that inasmuch as the hallmark of emptiness consists in the power of its deconstructive analysis, we can best appreciate such a deconstructive function by abandoning, once and for all, our ontological and epistemological preoccupations in the Western philosophical tradition that assumed a self-existent reality within and/or beyond the thoughts and objects of our mental and physical world. Instead, we can adopt a *pragmatic* approach that most effectively demonstrates the soteriological efficacy of emptiness. This is a welcome suggestion indeed. The pragmatic and contextual thrust in Huntington's hermeneutic methodology for Candrakīrti's Prāsangika-Mādhyamika is instructive and merits attention.

The sole function of emptiness, according to Huntington, is to completely strip away "the tendency to reify the screen of everyday affairs," so that practitioners can see things as they are. They are therefore "seeing through" the screen (illusion) "immediately given in everyday experience," which constitutes their intrinsic nature—namely, emptiness and dependent origination.[21] The "screen" here means perceptual, conceptual, and linguistic functions of the mind that are said to be responsible for the spiritual ignorance due to the reification of what they do. This results in a failure to see things clearly and leads consequently to clinging, aversion, and delusion. In view of this soteriological efficacy of emptiness which alone warrants ultimate truth, the worldly truth of everyday experience is regarded as illusory, and yet necessary for the ultimate truth. However, the two truths are ultimately incommensurable, while not mutually contradictory or exclusive. Huntington thus has this to say:

> An incommensurable truth and reality can be known only through contrast, and ultimately through direct experience, by first learning to identify and then totally to relinquish all obsession with our present observational language and the concepts and perceptions associated with it. . . .
>
> This does not mean that either conceptualization or perception can be denied outright, but that they must be transmuted through being placed in the larger context that is opened to view with the growing appreciation of an alternative, soteriological truth, a truth incommensurable with our normal ways of thinking and perceiving. It is at this point that we enter the sphere of the fourth and last noble truth: the truth of the path leading to the cessation of suffering for all living beings.[22]

To be sure, the worldly and ultimate truths do not represent two ontologically or epistemologically disparate realms. The ultimate truth is neither a something that manifests when the worldly truth is removed nor is it a nothing that is reified as the negation of the worldly truth. Nor does the worldly truth function as a "ladder" for climbing to a mystical union with the ultimate truth. This may be an accurate reading of Candrakīrti's early Indian Mādhyamika.

In any case, I wish to take issue for a moment with Huntington on his notion of "incommensurability" for the sake of our discussion, since the notion seems to exaggerate discontinuity between the two truths, so much so that it fails to see *continuity* between them. As a result, it makes it altogether impossible to establish a genuine internal relationship between them. In principle, I do not reject the notion of incommensurability as such. I do challenge, however, the very *efficacy* of such a notion in the soteriological project of Buddhism, as we follow Huntington's own pragmatic agenda.

In absence of any continuity, or intrinsic relationship, between the two truths, salvific possibilities for worldly truth cannot be sufficiently explored, and are almost nil at worst, even though we admit the fact that Candrakīrti's Prāsaṅgika-Mādhyamika does indeed have its own philosophical, ethical, and practical dimensions.[23] Furthermore, emptiness is confined only to its deconstructive function for ultimate truth, but cannot be dialogically and efficaciously engaged in the reconstructive function that involves worldly truth, because the investigation of everyday affairs as such is construed as not intrinsically conducive to the soteric aim of liberation. Thus emptiness suffers from a self-imposed, restrictive soteriology of ultimate truth; it is especially alienated from linguistic, conceptual, and rational experiences in daily life. Its all-or-nothing, nonnegotiable stance, which sternly refuses to call itself a view, also reduces all views to logical absurdity through the method of reductio ad absurdum. Thus there is no possibility for the worldly truth to partake in the ultimate truth, and vice versa. Put simply, there is an unworkable rupture between the secular and the religious. From Huntington's pragmatic standpoint, the issue not only has to do with Buddhism's efficacy in relation to Buddhists, but also poses a serious detriment to its efficacy in the secular world at large.

Needless to say, Dōgen was critical of abstract, theoretical aspects of Buddhist doctrines, including emptiness and the two truths. Even as a thinker, he was not a dharmologian per se like Nāgārjuna and Candrakīrti. (This remark in no way intends to imply that those classical dharmologians were strictly concerned with theoretical matters; in fact, they too were deeply practical and spiritual.) From the perspective of Dōgen's praxis orientation, the following few points are in order: (1) The deconstructive function of emptiness as ultimate truth lacks a dynamic, dialectical relationship with worldly truth. Consequently, its soteriological scope, hitherto unnecessarily constrained, should be expanded to include the reconstructive function of emptiness with respect to worldly truth, whose core in the Buddhist scheme lies in dependent origination. The two truths work most effectively and efficaciously as two foci in the realizational process. I have suggested this approach in the present work as a way to best appreciate Dōgen's Zen. They together orientate and conduce practitioners toward broader, deeper, and more precise salvific possibilities of realization. (2) Things and beings, activities and relations of worldly truth are seen in light of ultimate truth in such a way that they no longer hold the power to sway practitioners' lives, and the practitioners in turn attain the capacity to use them in salvifically wholesome ways. The emphasis in Dōgen's Zen thus deepens the meaning of "*seeing* things as they are" by construing it as "*changing/making* things as they are." This is precisely the point highlighted by "*expounding* a dream (or dream making) within a dream," in terms of the dynamic dialectics of equilibration and equilibrium in the steelyard analogy. (3) The deconstructive use of emptiness, however potent it may be, is alone not enough. The reconstructive use must be incorporated into it so as to make emptiness soterically full-fledged. How can emptiness be serene while constantly challenged by the turmoil of worldly truth? How can it be content with itself and not suffer with the world in its suffering? How can it be so free of vulnerability and ambiguity while endeavoring to be authentic in the context of temporal conditions? Is emptiness ever immune to "dim-sightedness?" Is it never "permeated" or "permeable" by "dim-sightedness"? Can we reclaim emptiness "in flesh and blood"? From Dōgen's standpoint, even "the emptiness of emptiness" should be examined in the deconstructive *and* reconstructive contexts through perpetually ongoing critical scrutiny.

7

At this juncture, the recent controversy of Critical Buddhism (*hihan Bukkyō*) that revolves around such ideas as *tathāgata-garbha* (*nyoraizō*), Buddha-nature, and original enlightenment (*hongaku*) is particularly relevant for our investigation. In the past two decades or so, it has stirred intense debate among scholars in Buddhist, Zen, and Dōgen studies on both sides of the Pacific. Hakamaya Noriaki and Matsumoto Shirō, Critical Buddhism's principal proponents at Komazawa University (Sōtō Zen) in Tokyo, jointly maintain the following general theses: (1) The Buddha-dharma should be seriously engaged in the exigent social and ethical problems of today, with an emphasis on the differences of existence, the critique of the uncritical acceptance of the status quo, and the practice of compassion. (2) Genuine Buddhism is comprised of criticism, no-self/selflessness, emptiness/dependent origination (temporal, karmic causation), impermanence, and faith. (3) There is an irreconcilable rupture between Mādhyamika thought on the one hand and Vijñapti-mātratā (Yogācāra) and *tathāgata-garbha* thoughts on the other; the former alone should be the central philosophy of Buddhism. (4) *Tathāgata-garbha* thought and its cognate doctrine, *hongaku* (original enlightenment) thought, are anti-Buddhist in that they are founded on the *ātman*-like substantialist view, being intrinsically authoritarian and discriminatory. (5) Those Buddhist schools/sects in East Asia, including Ch'an/Zen, that are rooted in *tathāgata-garbha* and *hongaku* thoughts, are, without exception, not Buddhism. (6) *Hongaku* thought was the ideology of the medieval religio-political power, and it legitimized Japanese ultra-nationalism and militarism of the modern period. It is still influential in contemporary Japan and manifests itself in such beliefs as ethnocentrism, cultural nationalism, and the polemics of Japanese uniqueness (*nihonjinron*).

(7) Dōgen's thought is radically different from Ch'an Buddhism of China
and is instead akin to Mādhyamika thought of Tibetan Buddhism. (8)
Dōgen's religion belongs to "the Buddhism of wisdom" (*chie no Bukkyō*)
with emphasis on *prajñā*, intellect, and language, not "the Buddhism of
meditation" (*zazen no Bukkyō*) with its emphasis on *dhyāna*, intuition, and
mysticism. (9) The pillars of Sōtō orthodoxy such as zazen-only (*shikan
taza*), "the wondrous practice of original enlightenment" (*honshō myōshu*),
and "the body-mind cast off" (*shinjin datsuraku*), all muddle-headed with
the *hongaku* way of thinking, are not essential to Dōgen's mature thought.
(10) In (Hakamaya's) comparative study of the seventy-five-fascicle and
twelve-fascicle texts of the *Shōbōgenzō*, the latter (the twelve-fascicle text)
has a more thorough, consistent anti-*hongaku* position and a more forceful
espousal of causality as compared with the former that shows ambiguities
and inconsistencies on the part of Dōgen. And (11) Dōgen's entire writings, especially the *Shōbōgenzō*, should be understood from his "definitive
viewpoint" in the twelve-fascicle text as normative. In light of this, his
success and failure, consistency and inconsistency, should be internally
determined.[24]

Broadly speaking, Critical Buddhism has served salutary purposes,
including intensifying debates on the relationship between Tendai *hongaku* thought and Dōgen's Zen; generating new sensibilities in the textual criticism of the *Shōbōgenzō* through the comparative analysis of the
seventy-five-fascicle and twelve-fascicle texts; arousing a heightened Buddhist awareness of contemporary social ills in Japan; and shaking up Sōtō
orthodoxy from its dogmatic slumber. More specifically, from the perspective of our investigation in the present work, I join Critical Buddhists in
underscoring the vital importance of such notions as emptiness, karmic
causation, temporality, the intellect, language, and criticism, in general
Buddhist discourse and particularly in Dōgen's thought. In terms of the
two truths of Mādhyamika philosophy, this means deep engagement in
worldly truth without losing sight of ultimate truth.

In a nutshell, Tendai *hongaku* thought was an affirmation of the
phenomenal world—including delusions, desires, and passions as well as
mountains, rivers, grasses, and plants—as absolute and nothing less than
the realization of buddhahood/original enlightenment itself, here and now.
It had two horns to its dilemma—duality and nonduality—that, when
translated into more concrete terms, consisted of the nullification of differences in the name of nonduality (equality) and the absolutization of
phenomena (the very differences) in the name of duality (differentiation).
These two contradictory perspectives fused into one, thereby constructing

the worldview that buddhahood/original enlightenment legitimized the phenomenal world absolutely. This was *hongaku* as doctrine in its simplest terms. At the same time, *hongaku* as ethos evolved into the powerful religious ideology of preordained harmony of the world and of radical this-worldly experientialism. The interplay of *hongaku* as the doctrine and *hongaku* as the ethos were inextricably interwoven in the subtly beautiful, yet potentially unsettling—Janus-faced, if you will—tapestry of the culture and mindset that was distinctively Japanese.

I am acutely aware of the rhetoric of some contemporary proponents of Japanism (*nihonshugi*) and the controversy of Japanese uniqueness (*nihonjinron*). In addition, I am fully sympathetic with Critical Buddhists' judgment on the complicity of the *hongaku* tradition with the religio-political power structure in medieval Japan as well as throughout Japan's history. Yet I am concerned that Critical Buddhist thinking strongly suggests a bent for "throwing the baby out with the bath water" with respect to the *hongaku* tradition as a whole. Let me illustrate my point: The medieval Japanese fascination, almost obsession, with "the surface" is integral to their religio-aesthetic sensibilities. William R. LaFleur observes this cultural trait:

> Shin'ichi Hisamatsu, recognizing that our ordinary rubrics of understanding tend to attribute more weight and value to what is "inside" and at the "core" and implicitly denigrate the outside as superficial, has astutely observed that Buddhism handles this by saying that "the true inside of the inside is not having inside or outside." In this extremely valuable formulation, Hisamatsu suggests that to dig to the core of the core is to discover the invalidity of such distinctions and also to discover that, seen from inside, the surface is deep. The terms are completely relative.[25]

Affective experience, however fleeting, is neither peripheral over against the center nor superficial as opposed to the core, let alone the means to the end. The so-called superficial appearance was infinitely fascinating and profound to the medieval Japanese. I think Dōgen identified with such a deep-rooted sentiment despite his cognizance of its ethically and religiously perilous implications, and did so without compromising critical discernment in accordance with emptiness. Thus, to use his expression, it amounts to saying: "The skin *is* the marrow." Note that the *is* here signifies intimacy—the mysticism of intimacy—that involves an extremely rich and complex fusion of ideas and sentiments. Dōgen was born into and imbibed the *hongaku* tradition and, throughout his life, struggled to negotiate his way *within* it, as well as *beyond* it. Instead of idealizing it, or abandoning it, or replacing it with another notion, Dōgen endeavored to see through it more clearly and penetratingly, by way of his religious method.

In view of these observations, it is one thing to conclude that the predestined harmony of existence and indiscriminate experientialism in question are inherently prone to the uncritical accession to the status quo; it is quite another to brand this single factor as the ideological root of social injustice, ethnocentrism, cultural chauvinism, and so on, as Critical Buddhists do.

Furthermore, Critical Buddhists stigmatize the *tathāgata-garbha* tradition as not Buddhism. Granted, there has been a persistent tendency on the part of a great number of dharmologians and practitioners in the history of the Mahāyāna to take *tathāgata-garbha* as if it were a substantialist notion. Even so, it is ultimately no more than a provisional designation (*kesetsu*; *prajñapti*). As such, it has the functions to orient, catalyze, and empower Buddhist practitioners in their salvific project, as effectively and efficaciously as possible.[26] It does not refer to any extralinguistic reality, hence it has nothing to do with the existence or nonexistence of its supposed referent. In short, *tathāgata-garbha* neither exists nor not exists. This is quite patent in view of the notion of emptiness in the Mahāyāna. At the same time, the issue of continuity and discontinuity between emptiness and *tathāgata-garbha* thoughts is extremely complex; I do not wish to dwell on this. All I wish to say at this point is that the issue is rooted in not only the doctrinal and dharmological ideas but the psychological, historical, and cultural conditions. Yet, by dismissing *tathāgata-garbha* thought in toto as un-Buddhist, Critical Buddhists scarcely delve into the *evolution* of the symbol in question in different cultures and histories, with different reasons for being. The point is that the evolution of a symbol does not strictly follow logical consistency; nevertheless, it does not follow from this fact that the symbol has no reason to exist. All in all, Critical Buddhism fails to appreciate the creative possibilities of the *tathāgata-garbha* tradition *in consonance with* the critical spirit of emptiness.

From the perspective suggested in particular in the present chapter, the problem with Critical Buddhism largely boils down to its restricted, elitist intellectualism, which it adopts as its *method*. In their reformist zeal, Critical Buddhists virtually banish meditation in favor of wisdom which is reduced to an intellect free of that which is fuzzy, spiritual, and obscurantist. This constrained intellectualist methodology has little or no empathy with the salvific needs and expressions of common religionists. It is highly legislative and exclusionary, rather than being open-ended and pluralistic. Its normative stance itself should be scrutinized in light of the broadest possible context of human experience and expression, for the sake of fairness. Unfortunately, the Buddhist soteriology that Critical Buddhists envision is a severely impoverished one.

By contrast, Dōgen, though no less cerebral, was temperamentally and methodologically "tender minded," while the Critical Buddhists are "tough minded," according to William James's expressions. He was simultaneously intellectual and visionary, critical and empathetic. His methodology combined understanding and criticism. As compared with this view, criticism for Critical Buddhists needs understanding based on a sound hermeneutics. What this means, in the final analysis, is that, while seriously engaged in worldly truth (in the scheme of Mādhyamika's two truths), Critical Buddhists are flawed in failing to sufficiently explore the reconstructive perspective of emptiness in Buddhist soteriology.

As noted before, Dōgen, confronted with the intellectual and cultural legacy of the *hongaku* tradition, carefully weighed its philosophical, ethical, and religious strengths and drawbacks, doing his utmost to surmount the dangers of its inherent substantialist proclivity and antinomian, fideist, and relativist implications. He constantly struggled within that tradition, neither flatly rejecting, nor wholeheartedly endorsing, nor directly or explicitly criticizing it. Despite this, his criticisms of the Senika heresy (*senni gedō*), "mind's eternity and form's perishability" (*shinjō sōmetsu*), and the naturalist heresy (*jinen gedō*), as well as a number of his passages in the *Shōbōgenzō*, unambiguously reveal his critical outlook on the *hongaku* way of thinking from the deconstructive perspective of emptiness.[27]

However, in my view Dōgen was not anti-*hongaku*—as Critical Buddhists make him out—any more than he was pro-*hongaku*.[28] He meticulously maneuvered his methodological and hermeneutic moves in his praxis-oriented soteriology to revolve around the two foci of the deconstructive and reconstructive ways of seeing/making emptiness. The upshot of this is what I call "critical (or radical) phenomenalism," in contrast to Hajime Nakamura's "absolute phenomenalism."[29]

8

In concluding this chapter, I wish to note that Dōgen went as far as possible given his limitations. Indeed, he went much further than Critical Buddhists in some respects, by tenaciously elucidating, penetrating, and refining the *reconstructive possibilities* of emptiness in such areas as language, thinking, and reason, as we shall review in the remaining chapters. In particular, his religio-philosophical and mythopoeic use of *hongaku*-related concepts and symbols, such as Buddha-nature, thusness, the dharma-world, the spatial conception of dependent origination, and the thought of enlightenment, are visionary and disciplined, yet never lose sight of the deconstructive tenor of emptiness.

Dōgen's method of "weighing emptiness" investigates "empty space's inside and outside" (*kokū no naige*), "empty space's [power] to destroy life and give life" (*kokū no sakkatsu*), and "empty space's worth and worthlessness" (*kokū no keijū*).[30] According to Dōgen, we weigh emptiness and things in this fashion to attain fairnes.

CHAPTER 4

The Reason of Words and Letters

I

As I have often noted in the present work and elsewhere, the single most original and seminal aspect of Dōgen's Zen is his treatment of the role of language in Zen soteriology. We moderns may pride ourselves on our acute language consciousness in the twentieth and twenty-first centuries, but Dōgen was no less aware. He is amazingly similar to us in this regard, and perhaps pushed beyond us by challenging not only his Buddhist contemporaries, but the modern world as well.

In the Mahāyāna, more specifically, Mādhyamika Buddhism, language does not refer to any fixed, self-existent, extralinguistic reality. Its functions and tasks are multiple and versatile so as to meet various human needs and interests. Although language may be limited to and bounded by sociolinguistic conventions, its limits and boundaries are provisional, open-ended, and impregnated with rich possibilities.[1] And yet, as noted before, those linguistic functions and tasks, according to the traditional Mādhyamika view, belong only to worldly truth, hence with limited values in relation to ultimate truth. Language intimates, but never is and cannot be intimate with, ultimate truth. The analogy of the "screen," according to Candrakīrti, must be stripped away once and for all in the name of liberation rather than, as in Dōgen, illumined and penetrated *discriminatively*, as part and parcel of liberation and ultimate truth. From Dōgen's perspective, Nāgārjunian disputations in terms of absolutism and nihilism would be grossly misguided.[2]

That said, brief highlights on Dōgen's view of language are necessary, to pave the way for our investigation in this chapter. First, note these statements:

What we mean by the sūtras is the entire universe itself. There is no space and no time that are not the sūtras. They use the words and letters of ultimate truth and the words and letters of worldly truth. They employ the language of gods and the language of human beings. They use the words and letters of beasts, those of *asuras*, and those of hundreds of grasses and thousands of trees. For this reason, the long and short, the square and round, the blue and yellow, the red and white—all of which marshall on in a dignified way throughout the universe in the ten directions—are undeniably the sūtras' words and letters and faces. These words and letters are all regarded as the instruments of the great Way and the scriptures for Buddhists.[3]

The monastics of future generations will be able to understand one-taste Zen (*ichimizen*) based on words and letters, if they devote their efforts to spiritual practice by seeing the universe through words and letters, and words and letters through the universe.[4]

As is clear from these quotations, the scope and depth of language are co-extensive and coeternal with those of the whole universe. Dōgen envisions the infinite varieties of linguistic modes according to different beings in the universe, in terms of "words and letters" (*monji*), "the sūtras" (*kyōkan*), and "expressions" (*dōtoku*). They are each unique and independent, yet depend on the other in line with the notion of dependent origination and are infinitely intertwined like vines. In Dōgen's methodological and hermeneutic vision, language is never construed as referential or representational, nor is the universe unchanging or self-sufficient. The linguistic modes are not related to each other hierarchically, teleologically, causally, logically, or in any manner prompted by metaphysical antitheses. As a pair of salvific foci, language and the universe in Dōgen's Zen are "ever intimate" (*shinzō*) in his mysticism of intimacy.

Second, the linguistic/expressive mode of each and every being, in Dōgen's view, is different from that of every other in a very unique fashion. Although these differences are unique, they are not atomistic and solipsistic to the extent that their uniqueness overrides the relationship of all the differences in their dynamics. Herein lie the possibilities of "communication" among different beings. A case in point, for example, is Dōgen's view of "insentient beings' discourse on the Dharma" (*mujō seppō*). Su Tung-p'o (1036–1101), a Sung poet, was awakened by the sounds of the stream in Lu-shan one night after having heard his Zen teacher, Chao-chio Ch'ang-tsung (1025–1091), expound the discourse of insentient beings on the Dharma. He immediately composed the following poem:

The sounds of the stream are [the Buddha's] long, broad tongue,
The sights of the mountains are his pure body.
Eighty-four thousand gathas throughout the night,
How can I expound them [to others] someday?

In the course of his commentary on this episode, Dōgen reasons: "Thus the stream sounds awaken Su Tung-p'o. Is this the workings of the stream sounds, or is it Chao-chio's discourse flowing into [the ears of Su Tung-p'o]? I suspect that Chao-chio's talk on insentient beings' dharma discourse, still reverberating, may have secretly intermingled with the nightly sounds of the streams."[5] What sort of linguistic alchemy (note "secretly intermingled with") is at work between "the nightly sounds of the streams," "Chao-chio's talk," and Su Tung-p'o's mind, so as to engender the "eighty-four thousand gathas" of the Dharma, in and through the poet's enlightenment? Dōgen's answer to this hypothetical question is minimal. Yet we can extract this much from his writings: Contrary to the deep-seated bias of humans, insentient beings do have the power to express themselves in their own ways and are boundlessly selfless in their efforts to communicate with us; this communication is possible only if we are equally as selfless.

Third, as Dōgen argues in his *Shōbōgenzō*, "Sansuikyō" (1240), the word *water* in its conventional usage is only one of the innumerable ways of naming that which is designated by *humans*. Water may be perceived as water by humans, but also as a palace by fish, as a jeweled necklace by gods, as bloody pus by hungry spirits, and so forth.[6] Dōgen also says this:

When we take a boat out on the ocean to a place where no mountains are visible and look around in the four directions, [the ocean] appears to be solely round, and no other features are apparent. This great ocean, however, is neither round nor square, and yet its qualities are inexhaustible. . . . Only insofar as our vision of the moment extends does [the ocean] appear temporarily to be round. The same holds true of the myriad dharmas. Although the world of dust and the world beyond illusion are pregnant with numerous aspects, we see and understand only according to our capacity for understanding. To understand the myriad dharmas' ways, we must know that, in addition to appearing as square and round, the other qualities of oceans and mountains are incalculable, and the various worlds are everywhere on all sides. Note that this is not only around us, but right beneath us—even in a single drop [of water].[7]

Dōgen's perspectival view of the world is apparent here. Even so, the relativity of all perspectives for Dōgen invariably implies the radical *relatedness* of all beings and all perspectives, not relativism. What he insists in the "Sansuikyō" fascicle with respect to water is, in the final analysis, that the word *water* must be *deanthropocentricized*, or dethroned if you will. Humans can see through "original water" which is empty of self-nature and in which all linguistic possibilities of different beings inform and liberate one another. By implication, the same recommendation applies to *all* forms of language. When Dōgen speaks of language, he always has such an "original language" in mind, and human language is understood in that context. The *radicalization* of language calls for a complete changeover of humanity's collective delusion and self-centeredness with respect to the nature and function of language.[8]

Fourth, for all its limitations, language can still function as the most powerful agent of salvific liberation. One of the clearest statements by Dōgen regarding language is stated in his critique of those Zen Buddhists who construed the irrationality of kōan utterances as the essence of Zen:

> In great Sung China today there are a group of scatterbrained people, whose number is so large that they cannot possibly be scared off by the faithful few. They argue: "Talks such as the Eastern Mountain's walking on the water, Nan-ch'üan's sickle, and the like are all incomprehensible utterances. Their import is that those talks which have to do with all sorts of discriminative thought do not belong with the buddha-ancestors' Zen talks. Only incomprehensible utterances are the talks of the buddha-ancestors. For this reason, Huang-po's training stick and Lin-chi's thundering shout exceed our comprehension, and have nothing to do with discriminative thought. They are thus regarded as great enlightenment before the origin of the universe. The past masters often employed as skillful means those phrases which cut off entangled vines, but their reason was that [such phrases] were incomprehensible."
>
> People who indulge in such nonsense have not met a true master yet, and lack the eye of proper study. They are fools not worthy of mention. . . . What those pseudo-Buddhists regard as "incomprehensible utterances" are incomprehensible only to them, not to the buddha-ancestors. Their lack of comprehension should never serve as an excuse for not studying the way of the buddha-ancestors' comprehension. Even if [those utterances] were in the end incomprehensible, what they [pseudo-Buddhists] now allegedly comprehend would still be wrong. Many such fellows abound in Sung China, and I have seen them myself. How pitiful are they who are unaware that discriminative thought *is* words and phrases and that words and phrases *liberate* discriminative thought![9]

Dōgen offers what I would call the "realizational" view of language, in contrast to the "instrumental" view that is epitomized in the Zen adage "the finger pointing to the moon" (*shigetsu*). This view is derived from the assumption that language has no intrinsic place in the salvific process of Zen, and accordingly, serves only as an instrument for the sake of enlightenment. His view pinpoints language as discriminative thought, and yet, as possessing the capacity to liberate discriminative thought. Let me make just two points here: (1) Language has a dual function—one is *limiting* and the other *liberating*. Is one a curse while the other a blessing? Is this oxymoronic? From Dōgen's standpoint, such questions smack of dualism, because both functions are capable of being soterically appropriated to serve as the bearer of realization. Both are necessary to one another; one without the other is vulnerable to the corrupting effects of language. (2) More significantly, however, "the way of the buddha-ancestors' comprehension" (*busso no riero*), as Dōgen contends, is such that, inasmuch as language is the core of discriminative thought, it has the power—perhaps the only power there is—to liberate it. Enlightenment, from Dōgen's perspective, consists of clarifying and penetrating one's muddled discriminative thought in and through our language to attain clarity, depth, and precision in the discriminative thought itself. This is enlightenment or vision.

Related to the preceding observations is that Dōgen's view of language is deeply grounded in his notion of temporality. His reasoning here is that if the cause of affliction and suffering lies in language, the way to release oneself from this predicament is in language itself. In fact, such a language-bound situation, Dōgen would suggest, is the only locus where one can attain realization. Dōgen thus focalizes language as the *agent* of liberation. It is small wonder then that, as we shall see presently, he meticulously explored and explicated the interior and exterior of language as the very fabric of existence and, hence, of his religion.

Fifth, this seemingly hyperintellectual stance on the part of Dōgen is not merely intellectual, because his "intellectualism" is invariably embedded in his praxis orientation. The praxis orientation is, in brief, epitomized by his notion of "total exertion" (*gūjin*), short for "the total exertion of a single thing" (*ippō gūjin*). When a single thing exerts itself totally and is cast off (*datsuraku*), it does so by virtue of and in concert with all other things of the universe. Thus a single dharma is "illumined," whereas all other dharmas are "darkened." When you talk about the self, all dharmas are "ever intimate" with the self, never erased, and the self and all dharmas are together cast off. As I wrote elsewhere: "A dharma is never juxtaposed to others; therefore, dharmas never oppose one another in a dualistic fashion. A dharma is, by definition, that particularity which transcends all forms of dualism; it is both independent of and harmonious with all dharmas."[10]

The same logic holds true of language: Words and letters, however socially constructed, are never mere signs in the abstract, theoretical sense, but alive and active "in flesh and blood." Contrary to the conventional view that language is no more than a means of communication, it is profoundly internal to an individual's life as well as to a collective life. Language flows individually and collectively through the existential bloodstream, so much so that it is the breath, blood, and soul of human existence. Herein lies the essence of Dōgen's radical phenomenalism (NB: Our discussion of *hongaku* thought in the previous chapter). Thus, language becomes *ascesis*, instead of *gnosis* or *logos*—"*seeing* things as they are" now means "*making* things as they are." In this light, the indexical analogy of "the finger pointing to the moon" is highly misleading, if not altogether wrong, because it draws on a salvifically inefficacious conception of language.

Sixth, in such a context, expression (*dōtoku*) signifies what is already expressed in a specific expression, what is not yet expressed, and what can be expressed—all simultaneously. The already expressed, the not yet expressed, and the expressible are dynamically related to one another within any given expression. Dōgen also employs another word *fudōtoku*, which means "that expression which is not or beyond expression" or "the inexpressible." Note that what is not/beyond expression is itself ultimately an expression, *not* an extra expressive substratum or reality. For Dōgen, the inexpressible is never reified as the opposite of expression. Thus, regarding the expressed and the inexpressible, Dōgen writes:

> When this expression is uttered, the inexpressible is not uttered. If you rec-
> ognize that expression is uttered in its fullness, and yet do not thoroughly
> verify the inexpressible as the inexpressible, that is still neither the original
> countenance nor the marrow-bones of the buddha-ancestors.[11]

What practitioners endeavor in Zen practice is to engage in a dialectical relationship between the already expressed and the not yet expressed/
the inexpressible, in search of the expressible. This is the dynamics of
expression.[12]

Incidentally, the dynamics and structure of expression in terms of
these foci show striking similarities to those of thinking, not-thinking and
nonthinking, which will be discussed in chapter 5. Given such similarities, nonthinking may be related to practitioners' sustained endeavors to
seek the expressible, namely, new expressive possibilities that are more
conducive to realization. This means practitioners are salvifically immersed

in perfecting their expression (and thinking) in their radical relatedness to all things of the world.

Dōgen demonstrated the foregoing principles of language himself in his practice of Zen, especially through his writing of the *Shōbōgenzō*. In doing so, he challenged and urged practitioners to do likewise—to critically reflect on how to practice their own religion for the sake of alleviating the suffering of all beings in the world, by authentically appropriating language in a specific situation. This, in essence, was the quest for the expressible.

2

Having set forth some salient features of Dōgen's view of language, I shall now examine, very schematically, some methods employed by Dōgen in his treatment of the kōan language in the realizational context. Discussed are seven classificatory topics: (1) Transposition of Lexical Components; (2) Semantic Reconstruction through Syntactic Change; (3) Explication of Semantic Attributes; (4) Reflexive, Self-Causative Utterances; (5) Upgrading Commonplace Notions and Using Neglected Metaphors; (6) The Use of Homophonous Expressions; and finally, (7) Reinterpretation Based on the Principle of Nonduality.[13] These headings should not be taken as rigid, self-contained categories; some examples cited may illustrate two or more of the above characteristics.

1. Transposition of Lexical Components

This is perhaps the most frequently used procedure in Dōgen's *Shōbōgenzō*. Its model consists of reshuffling the Chinese lexical components of a given phrase or expression, say, A, B, C, D, and E of "ABCDE" in Chinese, in order to adduce, for example, "BACDE," "ADCBE," and so on. The transposition of linguistic elements is intended to suggest that they are as dynamic and versatile as reality itself in their infinitely variegated configurations and possibilities. The analogy of a mosaic rearranged in multiple designs might help us here. Just as reality incessantly transforms itself, so can language act as a living force in its own right. The method of transposing lexical components attests to this view.

In his exposition on the Buddhist notion of "Mind itself is Buddha" (*sokushin zebutsu*), Dōgen presents a classic treatment. After defining the four linguistic elements—"mind" (*shin*), "itself" (*soku*), "is" (*ze*), and "Buddha" (*butsu*)—in "Mind itself is Buddha," he reshuffles them in various ways, and gives five examples out of twenty-four possible combinations.

> As for the "Buddha," it ["Mind itself is Buddha"] relinquishes all things and lets them go. Even so, it does not speak just in terms of [the Buddha's] sixteen-foot golden body.
>
> As for the "itself," it is the kōan that neither anticipates its realization nor averts its dissolution.
>
> As for the "is," it is the triple world that neither retreats nor advances; [as the triple world,] it is not mind-only.
>
> As for the "mind," it is walls and partitions; still, it is neither immersed in mud nor indulges in desires.
>
> [The buddha-ancestors] penetratingly study "Mind itself is Buddha," penetratingly study "Itself mind Buddha is," penetratingly study "Itself Buddha is mind," penetratingly study "Mind itself Buddha is," and penetratingly study "Is Buddha itself mind." Penetrating study such as this is indeed "Mind itself is Buddha," and exerting this, they have authentically transmitted ["Mind itself is Buddha"] to "Mind itself is Buddha." Such an authentic transmission has continued to this day.[14]

The Sōtō exegetical canon notes the twenty-four possibilities, but not their significance. Each lexical element represents a single dharma's total exertion that is absolutely discrete from all others, and that bears all others in it—without falling into atomism or monism. The same holds true of each and every combination of the four elements.

As often happens in the *Shōbōgenzō*, such modulated expressions cannot be easily rendered in intelligible statements. Perhaps Dōgen did not want them to be reduced to conventional locutions, but rather to be appreciated visually and aurally as they are, like the surrealistic images of a dream. Incidentally, this fanciful, even playful trait in Dōgen's diction has been largely overlooked by most Dōgen scholars. Far from being nonsensical constructs, such linguistic modulations stand for the infinite versatility of a seamless reality.

Closely related is Dōgen's inversion of lexical components—a technique that also reveals new signification. For instance, in his discussion of *tō higan* ("reaching the other shore"), Dōgen transposes its elements to create *higan tō* ("the other shore's arrival" or "the other shore has arrived").[15] Thus while the original meaning of *higan*, "the other shore"—that is, *nirvāṇa*, is clearly a future event attainable only at the end of countless kalpas of religious efforts, it is now radically transformed so that the other shore is no longer in the distance or in the future but the event of realization here and now.

2. Semantic Reconstruction through Syntactic Change

As we have already seen, Dōgen felt unconstrained by conventional Buddhist usage, and for that matter, by secular linguistic tradition. This is clearly demonstrated in his method of regrouping linguistic components in a sentence, often in violation of Chinese syntactic rules. Given the expression "A-B-CDE" in Chinese, for example, Dōgen would reorganize it as "AB-CDE," jolting the conventional meaning of the original. Alternately, he might just single out "BC." Meaningless in isolation from its original context, it would take on a novel signification with Dōgen. Thus he was a master of neologisms.[16] This technique involves the rearrangement of linguistic elements through syntactical reorganization (or disorganization) within an original passage.

In the "Busshō" fascicle Dōgen takes up the *Nirvāṇa Sūtra* passage *issai no shujō wa kotogotoku busshō ari* ("All sentient beings without exception have Buddha-nature") and shifts its syntactical components to read *issai shujō shitsuu busshō* ("All sentient beings, all existence, are Buddha-nature"). The far-reaching religious and philosophical implications of such distorted readings are now well known to us.[17] First, Buddha-nature as potentiality is construed as actuality, because sentient beings do not possess but *are* Buddha-nature; second, by being placed in apposition with "all existence," sentient beings are liberated from anthropocentrism as well as biocentrism; and third, "sentient beings," "all existence," and "Buddha-nature" are all nondually one—a notion that is described in a different context, but in a typically Buddhist locution, as "though not identical, they are not different; though not different, they are not one; though not one, they are not many."[18]

In his exposition on beholding the Buddha (*kembutsu*), quoting *moshi shosō wa hisō nari to mireba sunawachi nyorai o miru nari* ("If you discern that all phenomena are *not* phenomena, you see the Tathāgata"), Dōgen renders it as: *moshi shosō to hisō too mireba* . . . ("If you discern *both* all phenomena and non-phenomenon [simultaneously] . . . ").[19] Although the traditional reading stresses nondifferentiation as transcending or erasing differentiation, Dōgen's underscores differentiation as nondually one with nondifferentiation.

Dōgen's deliberate violation of Chinese syntactic rules, ordinarily considered essential to an accurate understanding of the original passage, is noteworthy in that not only was it deeply grounded in the enormously rich literary and religious tradition of medieval Japan, but his transgressive method was fully consistent with the logic of the expressible in his notion of expression (*dōtoku*), as noted before.

Related to the method of syntactic reconstruction (or deconstruction) is his "straight" reading of Sino-Buddhist expressions. A case in point: While *juki* is conventionally understood to be the Buddha's prediction of a disciple's future enlightenment, Dōgen transfigures it into the fact of that realization in the present. This is done by rendering the passage *masani anokutara sammyaku sambodai o ubeshi* ("You shall attain supreme, perfect enlightenment") as *tōtoku anokutara sammyaku sambodai* ("You have certainly attained supreme, perfect enlightenment").[20] The assurance of a future event is thus interpreted as the confirmation of a present one.

Elsewhere Dōgen renders *kono hō no okoru toki* ("When these dharmas arise") as *shihō kiji*. That is to say, *shihō* ("these dharmas") and *kiji* ("the time of their arising") are placed in apposition so that the entire expression now means: "These dharmas *are* the time of their arising." What he is referring to here is the nonduality of the *time* of arising and the *event* of dharmas: "[Speaking of 'When these dharmas arise,'] the 'time of arising' *is* 'these dharmas,' but it is not of the twenty-four hours of the day; 'these dharmas' *are* the 'time of arising,' yet they are not of the triple world arising in rivalry."[21] Dharmas do not move in time but are time; dharmas are not juxtaposed to one another spatially, nor is time segmental in temporal sequence. A simple phrase is therefore transformed into the keynote of Dōgen's religio-philosophical view of temporality—existence-time (*uji*).

3. Explication of Semantic Attributes

Dōgen's concern here is to probe the multiple meanings and functions of Chinese ideographs, by meticulously exploring the possible significations of a given character and experimenting with their soteriological possibilities. In doing so, he goes beyond the narrow confines of traditional diction and usage, penetrating the intricate interior of those significations.

The expression *kūge* originally meant in Buddhism "the flowers blooming in the sky" and, by extension, "illusory perceptions" or "unrealities." Yet, the word *kū* means not only "the sky" but also "emptiness," a pivotal notion in Mahāyāna Buddhism. Hence, at Dōgen's hands the term is metamorphosed from the illusory flowers to the evocative, powerful metaphor of "the flowers of emptiness."[22] With no definite demarcation between reality and illusion, all dharmas of the universe (including original enlightenment, original nature, and the like) thus become the flowers of emptiness. Dōgen writes:

There are indeed a number of ways to study the flowers of emptiness: Seeing by dim eyesight and seeing by clear eyesight; seeing by the Buddha's
eyesight and seeing by the ancestor's eyesight; seeing by the Way's eyesight
and seeing by the blind's eyesight; seeing in terms of three thousand years
and seeing in terms of eight hundred years; seeing from the perspective of
a hundred kalpas and seeing from the perspective of immeasurable kalpas.
Although these ways all see the "flowers of emptiness," the "emptiness" is
ever variegated, and the "flowers" ever manifold.[23]

It is worth noting that, as the last sentence of the above citation clearly
indicates, Dōgen's view of emptiness is thoroughly engaged with dependent origination so that it is invariably perspectival, individuated, and
polysemous.

Another significant character is *nyo*, which has the dual meaning of
"like" or "to resemble" on the one hand and "thusness" or "as-it-isness" on
the other. By using this twofold meaning, Dōgen maintains that likeness *is*
thusness in the nondual interfusion of the symbol and the symbolized, or of
worldly truth and ultimate truth. *Nyoze*, with its double meaning similar
to *nyo*, is also interpreted in this manner:

The "like" in the foregoing "like the moon in the water" means "the moon
in the water" itself. It is "the thusness of the water," "the thusness of the
moon," "in-thusness," and "the thusness of the in." We are not construing
the "like" as resemblance. "Like" *is* "thusness."[24]

Metaphors, similes, analogies, and parables, are, for Dōgen, not just the
vehicles for communicating an immediate experience or a truth, but the
bearers and workings of it. In this respect, language is the substance of
realization.

A similar utilization of the dual or multiple meaning of an expression also appears in the "Baika" fascicle, where *ima itaru tokoro ni* ("now
everywhere") is rendered as *nikon tōsho* ("the realized now is everywhere").[25]
The original passage is taken from Ju-ching's saying, "When Gautama
[the Buddha] sheds his [illusory] vision, the plum blossoms of just a single
branch are in the snow. Now everywhere thorns grow, but [the blossoms]
are smiling amid the spring breeze wafting madly all over."[26] By explicating its semantic attributes, Dōgen gives religio-philosophical ultimacy to
the quite ordinary words of "now everywhere."

Dōgen also transforms such an everyday phrase as *arutoki* ("at a certain
time," "sometimes," "there is a time," "once") into one of the most important notions in his Zen—*uji* ("existence-time"). This metamorphosis is

executed by way of changing its two components the *aru* and the *toki* into *u* ("existence," "being") and *ji* ("time," "occasion"), respectively, and recombining them as *uji* so that it unmistakably signals the nondual intimacy of existence and time.[27] Dōgen's new usage, moreover, adds a further dimension in terms of the realized now (*nikon*) with its rich connotations. Another common word *kyōryaku* ("to pass through," "to experience") is elevated to the status of a cognate notion signifying "the passage of time," by which Dōgen denotes "temporal dynamicity" or "temporal movement"—the dynamics of the realized present, in and through which all time and all existence are salvifically actualized. Temporal passage is stated succinctly:

> "Passage" is, for example, like spring. The spring has a great many features, and these are called "passage." We should study that the spring "passes" without anything outside itself. For instance, the "passage" of the spring always "passes through" the spring. The "passage" is not the spring but, because the spring is "that which passes," the "passage" now perfects the Way in [this particular] time of the spring.[28]

This last quotation is especially pertinent for our understanding of Dōgen's conception of language. As we have seen, language is as dynamically alive as any living being in the world. As such, the perspective which the concept of temporal dynamicity affords us is as pivotal within language as it is within our existence. In essence, the interior dynamics of words and letters amount to neither more nor less than the temporal dynamicity of existence-time.

4. Reflexive, Self-Causative Utterances

In Zen the statement of identity is quite commonplace and frequently used in order to suggest the nonduality of equality and differentiation, of emptiness and form, and so on. Underlying the statement of identity is the dialectical logic of identity-and-difference which appears in its classical form in the *Diamond Sūtra*.[29] Its paradigm can be stated as: "A is –A; therefore A is A." Thus "A" is at once negated and affirmed in a dialectical fashion, through the mediation and authentication of emptiness. Only then does "A" attain its authenticity.

Dōgen draws heavily on this kind of expression. Here are just two examples:

> The "emptiness" in question is not the "emptiness" of "form is emptiness."
> [The true meaning of] "form is emptiness" is not that you forcibly make

"form" into "emptiness" or that you split "emptiness" so as to fabricate "form"; it is the "emptiness" of "emptiness is emptiness." This "emptiness" of "emptiness is emptiness" is a single piece of rock in emptiness.[30]

An ancient buddha once said: "Mountains are mountains, waters are waters." This expression does not mean that we point to the mountains as the mountains, but that the mountains are nothing but the mountains. Therefore, we should study mountains penetratingly. When we study mountains penetratingly, that is the mountains' own efforts. Such mountains and waters become, of themselves, wise persons and holy sages.[31]

As is evident in these two quotations, the sayings "emptiness is emptiness" (*kū ze kū*), "mountains are mountains" (*san ze san*), and "waters are waters" (*sui ze sui*)—seemingly no more than ordinary tautological statements—forcefully and explicitly bear more realizational significance than any traditional readings. Dōgen makes his praxis orientation of the total exertion of a single dharma unequivocal in these illustrations.

By far the most Dōgen-like expression along these lines of thought, however, is made paradigmatically in this way: "Obstruction hinders obstruction, and sees obstruction; obstruction obstructs obstruction—such is time."[32] The original reads: *Ge wa ge o sae ge o miru. Ge wa ge o ge-suru nari, kore toki nari. Ge*, short for *keige* ("obstruction"), is used by Dōgen in his *Shōbōgenzō* in a way that deliberately distorts conventional usage. Instead of the dualistic "inter-dharmic" juxtaposition of that which obstructs and that which is obstructed, Dōgen employs the term to denote "intra-dharmic" dynamics in which that which obstructs and that which is obstructed are one and the same dharma.[33] As a consequence, *ge* or *keige* properly stands for the "self-obstruction" of a dharma—the *reflexivity* of salvific mode of being. This provides an excellent example of Dōgen's freehanded attitude toward the traditional mode of expression.

More importantly, however, Dōgen refuses to express a dharma's ultimate existence by any predicates other than its own self-referential expressions and activities, without denying its radical relatedness to all other dharmas.[34] Thus, as illustrated in the immediately preceding citation, a noun is converted into a makeshift verbal form in order to predicate that same noun: "obstruction obstructs obstruction." The paradigm "A A-s A" (e.g., "The sky sky-s the sky") and its variants appear numerously in the *Shōbōgenzō*:

Thought obstructs thought, and thereby sees thought. Expression obstructs expression, and thereby sees expression.[35]

[Water] is studied not only when humans and gods perceive water; there is the way of knowing in which water sees water itself. Because water enacts and realizes water, there is the way of experience in which water expresses water itself.[36]

As it works consummately, the great Way of all the buddhas is liberation and realization. Liberation means that life becomes transparent to life itself and death becomes transparent to death itself.[37]

Dōgen's predilection for creating new forms of verbs out of nouns is founded on such a dynamically reflexive supposition. He generates a seemingly endless multiplicity of new verbal expressions, all derived from nouns. It would not be a mistake to think that this procreation of verbs was greatly facilitated by the nature of the Japanese language that allows verbs to be formed from any nouns by adding the verbal suffix *su* or *suru* as in *dōtoku su* or *dōtoku suru* from *dōtoku*. Yet we should bear in mind that it was Dōgen's soteriological orientation that propelled him to take full advantage of this feature of the Japanese language. The *Shōbōgenzō* is replete with examples of this kind, of which I illustrate are but a few: *hōtō su* (from *hōtō*, "the jeweled pagoda"); *kokū su* (from *kokū*, "the empty sky"); *uji su* (from *uji*, "existence-time"); *jōroku konjin su* (from *jōroku konjin*, "the sixteen-foot golden body"); *kyōryaku su* (from *kyōryaku*, "temporal passage"); and *shitsuu su* (from *shitsuu,* "all existence").

5. Upgrading Commonplace Notions and Using Neglected Metaphors

Dōgen's sensitivity to language is also well demonstrated in his efforts to reinvigorate obsolete concepts and symbols with new potential, to revive forgotten metaphors from obscurity, to elevate denigrated words to new salvific status, to free expressions from their constraints and captivity, and to animate featureless words and images with new meanings. In all these cases, language is profoundly transfigured and given new life. His originality indeed consists in his ability to discover and rediscover the conceptual and symbolic possibilities of plain, unpretentious words and expressions, thus being not limited by traditional doctrinal categories as such.

The word *kattō* ("entwined vines") is usually given pejorative connotations that are associated with passions and desires, language and theories, all of which are regarded as entangling the mind in spiritual bondage. By contrast, Dōgen adopts this image to describe the type of communicative relationship between the master and the disciple—one that leads to ever greater discernment and understanding of the Dharma. He thereby not only gives it a positive significance, but advances its status to the level of the Dharma itself. He calls this "the reason that the skin, flesh, bones, and marrow entwine as vines" (*hiniku kotsuzui no kattō suru dōri*).[38] By implication, Dōgen suggests that the very texture of the Buddha-dharma is comprised of passions and desires, conflicts and differences. Reason cannot exist by freeing itself from such realities of the human condition any more than these realities can exist independently of the counsel of reason.

In a similar manner, Dōgen elevates *gabyō* ("the painted picture of a cake"), *kūge* ("the sky flowers"), *mitsugo* ("secret words"), and numerous other terms from their deprecatory status to a prestigious one in his universe of discourse. For instance, the *mitsu* in *mitsugo* now shifts its meaning from "that secrecy which is hidden" to "that intimacy which is transparent." Truth in this view is something to be clarified, not something to be uncovered. Furthermore, he minutely probes such conventional Buddhist locutions as *hiniku kotsuzui* ("the skin, flesh, bones, and marrow"), *gyōji* ("sustained practice"), *genjō kōan* ("the kōan realized in life"), *zenki* ("total dynamism"), *udonge* ("the udumbara flower"), *immo* ("thusness"), *arakan* ("the arhat"), *shoaku makusa* ("not to commit any evil"), in order to reclaim them from neglect and obscurity, so that they may function as transformative concepts and symbols in the soteriological milieu of the Buddha-dharma. Dōgen also radically reinterprets the concepts of *jinzū* ("supernormal powers"), *darani* ("charms and spells"), *tashintsū* ("the knowledge of other minds"), and *ōsaku sendaba* ("the ruler seeking the *saindhava*"), among many others.

A medieval aristocrat in origin, Dōgen could not help being literary and poetic in his writing. It is therefore not surprising that he also devotes his reflections to such emotive subjects as *baika* ("plum blossoms"), *kōmyō* ("the radiant light"), *tsuki* ("the moon"), *keisei sanshoku* ("valley sounds, mountain sights"), *shunjū* ("spring and autumn"), *ryūgin* ("a dragon's song"), and *sansui* ("mountains and waters"). A true alchemist of images and symbols, Dōgen evokes the vicissitudes of the dharmic drama of the universe through his exquisite, matchlessly poetic, and refined manipulation of them, without ever aggrandizing them. At his hand, they are regarded not as the means to edification but as the workings of ultimate truth itself. It is from this perspective that Dōgen may be seen to emphatically defy the traditional instrumental view of "the gate of skillful means" (*hōbemmon*) when he writes "The gate of skillful means is the supreme virtue of the buddha-fruition."[39] Therefore for Dōgen, "The Buddha-dharma, even in the figures of speech, is ultimate reality."[40] Those humble expressions adopted in Dōgen's symbolic universe are no exception in this regard.

6. The Use of Homophonous Expressions

In his writing, Dōgen frequently employs various associative tech- niques. Countless examples of poetic and ideational associations appear in the *Shōbōgenzō*. His associative use of homophonous pairs of expressions is especially well known, as in *Shobutsu kore shō naru yueni shobutsu kore shō nari* ("Because all the buddhas are of enlightenment, all things are of enlight- enment").[41] Dōgen adroitly and insightfully exploits the homophonous relationship between *shobutsu* ("all the buddhas") and *shobutsu* ("all things"). Consider another example: *Butsudō akiramezareba busshi ni arazu. Busshi to iuwa busshi to iu kotonari* ("Unless you understand the Buddha-way, you are not the Buddha's successor. The Buddha's successor means the Buddha's child").[42] Here Dōgen relates *busshi* ("the Buddha's successor") to *busshi* ("the Buddha's child"). Note that Dōgen chose the homophones in these cases and others not fancifully or rhetorically, but for the sake of clearer and deeper discernment.

The foregoing observations shed light on a recent hypothesis ad- vanced by Takasaki Jikidō. According to Takasaki, the phrase "the body-mind cast off" (*shinjin datsuraku*) never appears in Dōgen's master Ju-ching's works. Another expression "the mind's dust cast off" (*shin- jin datsuraku*), however, does appear just once. It is possible, Takasaki thus reasons, that Dōgen might have misread Ju-ching's "the mind's dust cast off" as "the body-mind cast off."[43] When we consider the fact that these two expressions are homophonous in Japanese, and place this fact in the context of Dōgen's frequent use of homophonous expressions, it is not too farfetched to suppose that he discovered the central idea of "the body-mind cast off" by way of homophonous association, which in turn triggered his religio-philosophical imagination. If this conjecture is cor- rect, we may further speculate that Dōgen's proclivity for creative mis- reading might have been inspired early on in his student years in China (1223–1227).

Regardless of the validity of such a surmise, there is no doubt about Dōgen's superb mastery of the associative technique as a means of further- ing religious understanding.

7. Reinterpretation Based on the Principle of Nonduality

If there is any single principle central to Dōgen's Zen, it is that of emptiness, as appropriated in the context of realization in terms of the dynamic interplay of duality and nonduality, or of worldly truth and ultimate truth. Let us look at some examples of Dōgen's radical reinterpretation of nonduality in the aforementioned context of emptiness, which can be conveniently grouped under eight headings: (i) The relative seen in terms of the ultimate; (ii) the future construed as the present; (iii) the transcendental/static interpreted in terms of the realizational/dynamic; (iv) different stages of practice conceived as all alike full-fledged enlightenment; (v) a preenlightenment event viewed as a postenlightenment one; (vi) imperative statements construed as declarative ones; (vii) analogy seen in terms of identity; and (viii) interrogatives and negatives used in the context of realization. Instead of providing illustrations for each heading, I shall limit myself to just a few representative cases.

Dōgen writes:

> To say "if the time arrives" is tantamount to declaring that the time has already arrived. How can you doubt this? You may entertain a doubt about the time. Be that as it may, witness Buddha-nature's arrival. Know that, [as you understand] "if the time arrives" [in this way], every moment of the twenty-four hours of the day does not pass by in vain. The "if-arrives" (*nyakushi*) means the "already-arrived" (*kishi*). [Otherwise,] "if the time arrives" would mean "Buddha-nature never arrives." For this reason, since the time has already arrived, Buddha-nature is unmistakably present here and now.[44]

The conventional reading of "if the time arrives," according to which Buddha-nature is to be realized sometime in the future, is transformed so that Buddha-nature is already actualized in the present.

In the "Tashintsū" fascicle Dōgen deals with the incident of Nan-yang Hui-chung (d. 776) and Ta-erh, a dharma master from India, in which the former tests the authenticity of the latter's ability to know others' minds (i.e., one of the six supernormal powers). But Dōgen criticizes the popular dualistic understanding of this power, interpreting it instead in such a way that it is now conceived to be the discernment of and penetration into that ultimate mind, which overcomes the dualisms of self and other and of body and mind, within the relative realm. That is, the supernormal power of knowing others' minds is interpreted in the context of the nonduality of self and other and of body and mind.[45]

Discussing Bodhidharma's expression "the skin, flesh, bones, and marrow" (*hiniku kotsuzui*), Dōgen repudiates the traditional view, which sees these four as the progressive stages of understanding or as the way of hierarchically ranking Bodhidharma's four disciples, Tao-fu, Tsung-chih, Tao-yü, and Hui-k'o. Instead, he views them from the ultimate perspective of realization:

> You should understand that the [first] ancestor's words "the skin, flesh, bones and marrow" are not concerned about shallowness and deepness [in the disciples' understanding]. Even though there are superior and inferior views, the ancestor's words each signify solely the attainment of his whole being. Their cardinal meaning is that the attainment of marrow, the attainment of bones and so on are to guide people; there is no sufficiency or insufficiency in holding grass or dropping grass [as a means to guide people according to their abilities and needs]. . . . What [Bodhidharma] said of the four disciples is that each was equal from the beginning. Although the ancestor's words are the same, the four views are not necessarily identical. . . . The skin, flesh, bones, and marrow partake equally in the first ancestor's body-mind. The marrow is not deepest; the skin is not shallowest.[46]

The following example has to do with the well-known story of Nan-yüeh's polishing a tile, which was mentioned earlier:

> When Chiang-si Ma-tsu formerly studied under Nan-yüeh [Huai-jang], Nan-yüeh personally granted the seal of the mind to him. This is the beginning of [the tradition of] tile polishing. Subsequently, Ma-tsu resided in the Ch'uan-fa yüan, doing zazen daily for some ten years. . . . One day when Nan-yüeh visited Ma-tsu's hut, Ma-tsu attended to him. Nan-yüeh asked: "What have you been doing lately?" Ma-tsu replied: "These days I am just doing zazen." Nan-yüeh: "What is doing zazen for?" Ma-tsu: "I strive to make a buddha." Then Nan-yüeh picked up a tile and began to polish it against a rock near Ma-tsu's hut. Seeing this, Ma-tsu immediately asked: "Reverend, what are you doing?" Nan-yüeh: "I am polishing a tile." Ma-tsu: "What is polishing a tile for?" Nan-yüeh: "I am going to make a mirror by polishing it." Ma-tsu: "How can you make a mirror by polishing a tile?" Nan-yüeh: "How can you make a buddha by doing zazen?"[47]

In this quotation and his subsequent exposition in the "Kokyō" fascicle, Dōgen assumes that the incident took place *after* Ma-tsu received the seal of the buddha-mind from Nan-yüeh. The original source of the story, however, presented the two events in reverse order.[48] In other words, what Dōgen suggests above is the story of the two masters' exchange of words and acts on the subject of making a buddha and doing zazen as the postenlightenment encounter. Consequently, the thrust of the story now is the nonduality of tile and mirror and of zazen and buddhahood—no longer the unbridgeable chasm between them. When the means-end and all other models of relationships collapse, the focus is then the ongoing process/practice of sitting, polishing, and making that is the very evidence of buddhahood. Precisely herein lies enlightenment (*shō*).

3

Let me conclude this chapter by recapitulating a few points:

1. In Dōgen's religio-philosophical milieu, the interior and exterior of language constitutes the very fabric of all existence. As such, language is appropriated as central to the salvific realization of his Zen. For that reason, Dōgen explores language inside out and scrupulously experiments with it. He challenges its conventional locution with a view toward creating a more humane, compassionate world. In his *Shōbōgenzō*, he typically repeats a certain concept, metaphor, or image, changes word order, shifts syntax, creates new expressions, indicates alternate meanings, resuscitates forgotten or dead symbols, and so on. He reads Buddhist scriptures, treatises, Zen classics, and other texts in his specific manner, from his unique perspective, and with his critical acumen.

Indeed, every reading is at once deconstructive and reconstructive in Dōgen's methodological and hermeneutic process. In a characteristically Buddhist way, he would say that deconstruction and reconstruction as a pair of two foci are nondual—different and identical simultaneously. Yet, what distinguishes Dōgen's reading or misreading is that, through the linguistic manipulations of methods and principles at his disposal, he exemplifies them as soteric practice; this is in essence the practitioner's responsibility to reexpress the expressed in terms of the expressible, as informed by the inexpressible.

2. Language must meet the challenges of these two concerns: (i) To overcome the sociolinguistic and anthropocentric limitations of the human language and thereby open it up to the horizons of new possibilities beyond human consciousness, and (ii) to deeply penetrate the human condition so that practitioners may understand and be liberated from suffering and delusions, by way of dualities such as conflicts, contradictions, and ambiguities, as well as by way of reflective and critical thinking, especially in ethical matters. From Dōgen's standpoint, language should not evade these two concerns and their challenges. In the dynamic, dialectical relationship

between them (as the foci) lies Zen realization. In this manner, while inevitably couched in human language, and thus still embedded in temporality and existentiality, Dōgen's methodology frees itself from reductionism on the one hand and absolutism on the other.

3. Language, thinking, and reason constitute the key to both zazen and kōan study within Dōgen's praxis-oriented Zen. The kōan's and zazen's function is not to excoriate and abandon the intellect and its words and letters, but rather to liberate and restore them in the Zen enterprise. In short, enlightenment is not brought about by direct intuition (or transcendent wisdom) supplanting the intellect and its tools, but in and through their collaboration and corroboration in search of the expressible in deeds, words, and thoughts for a given situation (religious and secular). Zazen and kōan in this respect strive for the same salvific aspiration of Zen. The language of the old-paradigm kōan (*kosoku kōan*) becomes a living force in the workings of the kōan realized in life (*genjō kōan*). With their reclaimed legitimacy in Zen, language, thinking, and reason now enable practitioners to probe duality and nonduality, weigh emptiness, and negotiate the Way. Method and realization, rationality and spirituality, thinking and praxis, go hand-in-hand in Dōgen's Zen. Such is "the reason of words and letters" (*monji no dōri*).

CHAPTER 5

Meditation as Authentic Thinking

I

Meditation and thinking are among the most vexatious subject matters in Zen Buddhism, specifically in Sōtō Zen. Within the Sōtō tradition, the mainstream view holds that seated meditation in terms of zazen-only (*shikan taza*) is the foundation of what its upholders call "Dōgen Zen,"[1] either transcendentalizing or minimizing thinking; as a result, thinking has been almost incapacitated in the tradition. On the other hand, Critical Buddhism, as touched on before, radically challenges the orthodox veneration of zazen-only and its kindred notions as the sine qua non of Dōgen's religion, which its proponents insist is to be read strictly in terms of wisdom/intellect (*prajñā*), not meditation (*dhyāna*). Dōgen's alleged anti-*hongaku* stance is also read as the norm.[2] From very early on in Buddhist history, there have been tensions between the bhaktic and gnostic approaches, as well as between the samādhi-oriented and prajñā-oriented ways;[3] also well known are those between the doctrinal/scriptural and meditational schools in Chinese Buddhism, and between silent-illumination zen (*mokushō-zen*) and kōan-introspection zen (*kanna-zen*) in Ch'an/Zen. In view of this, the recent controversy within Sōtō Zen may not be so surprising. It nevertheless is indicative of the potential for the issue of meditation and thinking to arouse an intense controversy as never before. Indeed, they are still odd bedfellows today more than ever.

On this issue, where did Dōgen himself stand? To what extent was he the meditator of zazen-only? Was zazen-only just zazen only to him? In his *Shōbōgenzō* why does Dōgen the meditator seem to recede to the background, whereas Dōgen the thinker comes to the foreground? If this impression is correct, is it to be regarded as ironic? Did Dōgen the thinker dispense with zazen altogether and devote himself to writing the *Shōbōgenzō*? Unfortunately, textual and historical studies of Dōgen do not provide fully satisfactory answers to these questions. Even so, a clue to them seems to lie in his concept of nonthinking (*hi-shiryō*), along with those of thinking (*shiryō*) and not-thinking (*fu-shiryō*). What then does Dōgen mean by nonthinking?

In recent Dōgen/Zen studies, some scholars have attempted to explore the notion of nonthinking. For example, Izutsu Toshihiko, generally in line with D. T. Suzuki's radically intuitionistic approach to Zen, insists upon "mistrust in thinking" and "elimination of discursive thinking" quite explicitly, because thinking is the most serious impediment to spiritual realization. He further suggests a thinking ("A-thinking," "a-thinking thinking") that operates in a totally different form and at quite a different level of consciousness from the one we are familiar with in our daily experience; it is activated by wiping out all images, ideas, and concepts from one's consciousness—by opening up to the primordially undifferentiated as the ground of all things prior to their differentiation. This undifferentiated is not a blank slate of consciousness, but mindfulness, through which one engages in thinking in the subliminal regions of the mind, thereby enabling one to attain metaphysical knowledge of Being ("pure Existence," "the very plenitude of Being"). It is "the metaphysical ground of Being itself which remains eternally untouched by the stream of images and concepts that pass across the empirical plane of consciousness." Izutsu's view is monistic, essentialistic, universalistic, and borders on a form of perennial philosophy. Concepts and images are nothing more than the bottom rung of the ladder for a heroic climb to the top of Being itself.[4]

On the other hand, Abe Masao, in keeping with the tradition of Akiyama Hanji and other philosophers in Dōgen studies in Japan, offers a measured, nuanced reading of nonthinking, which he says constitutes the intellectual pivot of Zen:

> Zen does not establish itself on the basis of either thinking or not-thinking, but rather *non*-thinking, which is beyond both thinking and not-thinking. When not-thinking is taken as the basis of Zen, anti-intellectualism becomes rampant. When thinking is taken as the basis, Zen loses its authentic ground and degenerates into mere conceptualism and abstract verbiage. Genuine Zen, however, takes non-thinking as its ultimate ground, and thus can express itself without hindrance through both thinking and not-thinking, as the situation requires.[5]

In the same vein, Abe writes elsewhere:

> Non-thinking is a position which transcends both relative thinking and relative not-thinking. Indeed, for that very reason, Zen non-thinking is

unshackled ultimate thinking. Therefore, it transcends thinking in the usual sense. This does not mean a simple lack of understanding in respect to thought. It is rather based on a fundamental critique of the nature of thinking asserting that human thinking is essentially a substantive one.[6]

At the same time, from the standpoint of thought and action, nonthinking is construed as nonattachment; in this sense it is "Non-abiding Origin."[7] Abe's view of nonthinking then amounts to that thinking which is free of substantialism and attachment.

The problem with Abe's interpretation, as far as I am concerned, has primarily to do with not what he has said so much as what he has not said. Among other things, the major thrust of his nonthinking lies in *transcending* (relative) thinking and (relative) not-thinking, but he mentions little or nothing about nonthinking as *mediating* (revaluated) thinking and (revaluated) not-thinking in their dynamic, dialectical relationship in concrete everyday situations. Without such an engaged, catalytic role within the temporality of the human condition, nonthinking would still be in the abstract, and hence insufficient and inefficacious.

There are other thinkers who have offered interpretations of nonthinking similar to Izutsu's and Abe's. By and large, these interpreters are comparative philosophers whose analyses tend to be formalistic, formulaic, and static, resulting largely in metaphysicized readings of Dōgen's texts.

2

These essential passages on the notion of nonthinking, with Dōgen's brief commentary, appear at the very beginning of the *Shōbōgenzō*, "Zazenshin" (1242):

Once Great Teacher Yüeh-shan Hung-tao was sitting [in meditation], and a monastic asked him: "What are you thinking in that resolute state [of seated meditation]?" The teacher replied: "I am thinking through not-thinking." The monastic then asked: "How do you think through not-thinking?" The teacher said: "[By way of] nonthinking."

Realizing such utterances of the Great Teacher's, we should study resolute sitting and transmit it correctly, which means the thorough investigation of resolute sitting handed down in the Buddha-way. Although he is not the only person [who taught] thinking in the resolute state, Yüeh-shan's utterances are the very best because of his "thinking through not-thinking." [Thus] thinking is the skin, flesh, bones, and marrow [of zazen]; likewise, not-thinking is the skin, flesh, bones, and marrow [of zazen].

The monastic said: "How do you think through not-thinking?" Although not-thinking is indeed time-honored, [he cross-examines it] refreshingly [with the question], *"How do you think?"* Can there be no thinking in the resolute sitting? How can you fail to understand the resolute state and beyond? Unless you are a short-sighted fool, you should have the capacity, in addition to the thinking, to question and reflect on such a resolute state.

The Great Teacher replied: "[By way of] nonthinking." The use of nonthinking is unmistakable, and yet to think through not-thinking, we always exert nonthinking. There is "someone" in nonthinking, and this someone sustains the one [who sits in zazen]. Although it is one's self who sits resolutely, [this sitting] is not merely thinking but exerts itself as the resolute sitting. Resolute sitting sits resolutely; if so, how could this resolute state think of itself [as its object]? For these reasons, the resolute state of sitting is neither of the measure of the Buddha nor of the measure of the Dharma, neither of the measure of awakening nor of the measure of comprehension.

From the outset, we must guard ourselves against the common thesis of some conventional interpretations that states thinking and not-thinking are either epistemological or ontological antitheses, instead of being a pair of soteric foci free of substantialist moorings whose bifurcation is to be overcome. On the one hand, thinking is conceived as functions of consciousness, such as perceptions and conceptions, or activities of the intellect, such as reasoning, comparison, and classification. What Buddhists call discrimination or discriminative knowledge (*fumbetsu*; *fumbetsu-chi*) broadly covers these activities of the mind that are often associated with delusions and afflictions. On the other hand, not-thinking is viewed as the negation of such discriminations so that it affirms a transcendent cognition beyond concepts and images, which in Buddhism is called non-discriminative knowledge (*mu-fumbetsu-chi*). Along this line of thought then, nonthinking is regarded as that thinking which casts off the antitheses of thinking and not-thinking and, accordingly, is transcendent and unattached.

The problem with such a reading, however, is that both thinking and not-thinking are relativized as abstract opposites to be superseded by nonthinking. The relativization of thinking and not-thinking is as bad as the absolutization of them. Its net result is essentially a metaphysical privileging, if not an absolutization, of nonthinking. Somewhere along the way, thinking, not-thinking, and nonthinking have lost the *dialectical dynamicity* of their salvific functions. As a result, the so-called *unattached* thinking has unwittingly become disembodied and impotent.

3

In his writings, Dōgen employs a number of notions that broadly denote discriminative thinking—*nenryo, nenkaku, ryochi, ryochi nenkaku, chikaku, fumbetsu, shiyui, shiryō*, and so on, although they vary in their connotations and nuances. The common thread running through them is the activities of consciousness and the intellect that "divide" and "split" the seamless reality. He often uses those terms, without adding negative qualifiers, in order to designate negative significations. At the same time, he also uses them with unambiguously negative qualifiers, as in such phrases as *ja shiryō* or *ja shiyui* ("fallacious thinking"), *aku shiyui* ("bad thinking"), *mō fumbetsu* ("delusory discrimination"), and the like. Nowhere does Dōgen, however, construe discriminative thinking as negative aside from its context, as we might expect in view of the fact that the word "discrimination" is all too often used pejoratively in Zen discourse. He even adopts the expression "correct discrimination" (*shō fumbetsu*).[8] The point here is that Dōgen generally employs thinking in the sense of *revaluated* thinking in the salvific milieu.

Perhaps the most illuminating passage in this connection appears toward the end of the *Shōbōgenzō*, "Zazenshin," where Dōgen comments on the *Tso-ch'an chen* (Admonitions for Seated Meditation) by Hung-chih Cheng-chüeh (1091–1157). Hung-chih's passage is given here in part:

> The essential function of all the buddhas,
> The functioning essence of all the ancestors:
> It knows without touching things,
> It illumines without depending on causes.
> . . . .
> Knowing without touching things,
> Its knowledge is inherently subtle.
> . . . .
> Its knowledge inherently subtle,
> It is ever without discriminative thinking.
> . . . .

Dōgen's commentary follows immediately after these lines:

> Thinking is itself knowing, without any dependence whatsoever on another's power. Its knowing has its form; its form is the mountains and rivers. These mountains and rivers are subtle, and this subtlety is wondrous. When we put it to use, it is lively and spirited. In order to become a dragon, it

does not matter [to a fish] whether it is inside or outside the Yü Gate. To put this single knowing even to the slightest use, we exert the mountains and rivers of the entire world and know them with our utmost. Without intimacy between our knowing and the mountains and rivers, not a single knowing or a half understanding on our part will be possible. We should not deplore the late arrival of discriminative thinking. The buddhas, who are "ever already" discriminative [in their thinking], have already been realized. [Hung-chih's] "ever without" means "ever already," and "ever already" means realization. This is why [Hung-chih's] "ever without discrimination" means you meet not a single person.[9]

Note, among other things, that in the manner of his now celebrated linguistic transformations of some traditional expressions, Dōgen translates "ever without discriminative thinking" (*sōmu fumbetsu*) into "ever already discriminative thinking" (*isō fumbetsu*), thus identifying discriminative thinking with original realization. The *sō* in *sōmu* and *isō* has such meanings as "once," "formerly," and "ever," and Dōgen appropriates the *sō* here to mythopoetize—not metaphysicize nor substantialize—the timeless origin. This is illustrated, for example, by Ta-chien Hui-neng's (638–713) "the original countenance before one's mother and father were born." As noted before, a similar usage is apparent in the expression *shinzō* (in which *zō* is the corruption of *sō*) to connote "ever intimate."[10]

Instead of reading the "ever without" in its conventional sense, Dōgen transforms it in such a way that discrimination is "ever already" active and vibrant throughout the realizational process. The underlying assumption is preeminently Buddhist: If the cause for the arising of our predicament lies within discrimination, then the cause for the eradication of such a predicament also lies within that discrimination itself, not outside.[11] Discriminative thinking, delusory though it may be, possesses an intrinsic capacity within itself to overcome and transform its own limitations, for it is "ever already" within the process of realization itself, not "ever without." That is why discriminative thinking neither arrives nor leaves.

To Dōgen's credit, delusion and enlightenment *alike* are rooted in discriminative thinking. Like it or not, you are bound to discriminate and differentiate things, events, and relations, in a myriad of different ways. The activities of discrimination may be self-centered, discriminatory, and restrictive. Yet, discriminative activities, once freed of substantialist, egocentric obsessions, can function compassionately and creatively. Thus there are two kinds of discriminative thinking at an existential level, delusive and enlightened. To Dōgen, whether or not we use discrimination in the Zen salvific project is not the issue; rather, how we use it is. Both the rational and the irrational originate from discriminative thinking, as do the rational and nonrational. (More will follow on this matter later.) Here, Dōgen takes exception to the traditionalist Zen view that uncritically negates thinking on the grounds of discrimination.

We are now in a better position to appreciate Dōgen's statement such as this:

> To arouse the thought of enlightenment, one always employs the mind of discriminative intellect. . . . Without this discriminative intellect, the thought of enlightenment cannot be aroused. We do not construe the discriminative mind as the thought of enlightenment itself, but we arouse the thought of enlightenment through this mind of discriminative intellect.[12]

Certainly Dōgen would not permit a reductionist path that privileges the activities of the human intellect as objective and rational, and thereby relegates all other activities of the mind beyond its pale to mere subjectivity and irrationality outside knowledge and cognition. Nor would he allow a teleological path in which the discriminative mind is instrumental in causing the thought of enlightenment, for, as Dōgen writes elsewhere, the thought of enlightenment *arises* and this arising constitutes *arousing* it.[13] Dōgen might appear to us here as if he were delicately distancing himself from both holistic and reductionistic pitfalls in our contemporary terms. However, his intellectual astuteness should be located in a larger soteriological context.

Thus viewed, the thought of enlightenment, often interpreted in Buddhism as the incipient aspiration for enlightenment, is neither a condition antecedent to, nor an awareness inferior to, enlightenment. Instead, it is *full* enlightenment pure and simple; as such, it functions at the beginning, middle, and end of enlightenment. It follows from this that discriminative thinking invariably works together with the thought of enlightenment, all through the practitioner's practice. Thinking is now free from an overly constrictive view of reason and thinking, and accordingly, it serves in a way that is responsive to the conditions and needs of any given religious situation.

It is against this background of Dōgen's expansive view on thinking's mythopoeic boldness and versatility that we can properly understand his seemingly fantastic ideas and utterances about it. We have already cited above:

> Thinking is itself knowing, without any dependence whatsoever on another's power. Its knowing has its form; its form is the mountains and rivers. These mountains and rivers are subtle, and this subtlety is wondrous. . . .

> Without intimacy between our knowing and the mountains and rivers, not
> a single knowing or a half understanding on our part will be possible.

Thinking is not only polymorphous, but also intimate in a very special
sense. Consider also his discussion of one of the four modes of supranormal
power (*jinsoku*), the one that is attained through thinking (*shiyui jinsoku*):

> The mode of supranormal power attained through thinking is of the bud-
> dha-ancestors, with the karmic consciousness that is vast and giddy, with-
> out any fixed ground. There are the body's thinking, the mind's thinking,
> consciousness's thinking, a straw sandal's thinking, and thinking of one's
> self prior to the kalpa of nothingness.[14]

From the mind's thinking to the body's thinking, from a straw sandal's
thinking to thinking of one's self prior to the kalpa of nothingness, all
innumerable variations of thinking are (1) executed by the totality of the
body-mind and beyond; (2) embedded in the "karmic consciousness that is
vast and giddy" (*gosshiki bōbō*); (3) "without any fixed ground" (*muhon kakyo*);
and (4) possible in and through "intimacy" between thinking/knowing and
its form (e.g., the mountains and rivers). What is significant for us in the
present context is that, regardless of its modes, thinking is firmly inherent in the karma-ladenness and time-boundness of existence. In addition,
in the final analysis, there is no escape from such existentiality. And yet,
Dōgen's soteriological project contends that the way to redeem the karma-
laden, time-bound nature of thinking lies within that nature itself—that
is the paradox and mystery of the human condition. From this perspective,
thinking is now free to be responsible, disciplined, fair, and compassionate in one's personal morality and social ethical thought and, furthermore,
is even free to roam playfully throughout the universe in its mythopoeic
imagination.

This is exactly what Dōgen did in his Zen. And this is why I have
previously observed that Dōgen was radically existential and visionary at
the same time. To him, thinking is malleable, adaptable, and resilient in
accordance with one's vision of salvific possibilities.

Along this line of thought, thinking is also said to be exerted by
"the mind of the entire great earth" (*jindaichi no kokoro*), by "the mind of
trees and stones" (*bokuseki shin*),[15] by "the mind of the mountains and rivers and the great earth" (*senga daichi shin*), by "the mind of the sun, moon,
and stars" (*nichigetsu seishin shin*),[16] and by "the one mind of all dharmas"
(*issaihō isshin*).[17] Elsewhere Dōgen uses the expression "thinking of the ten
directions" (*jippō shiyui*).[18] All these locutions are not the whims of fantasy.

On the contrary, Dōgen's mystic vision situates thinking firmly in the context of the existentiality and temporality of the human condition. Better yet, the logic of intimacy between the self and the universe in terms of thinking is indelibly part and parcel of Dōgen's Zen.

4

What is not-thinking?

Not-thinking may be construed as a state or realm in which all thinking is extinguished and all mental activity is absent. Take, for example, "the attainment of cessation" (*nirodha-samāpatti*) in the Theravāda tradition.[19] This state of extinction is said to be reached by the meditator upon the successful completion of the sphere of neither-perception-nor-nonperception, the last of the eight jhānic (transic) paths. In such a state, the meditator's verbal, mental, and bodily functions come to a standstill. Though life is not exhausted, there is an awareness of a fullness of experiential quality, often identified with *nibbāna*. The ultimacy of cessation in Buddhist soteriology has been claimed by many Buddhists in Theravāda countries throughout Buddhist history. Nevertheless, its precise salvific status and role are much debated and remain problematic. This debate includes such issues as (1) whether it is a species of annihilationism (one of early Buddhism's two extreme views, the other being eternalism);[20] and (2) if it is realizable at all, and whether its form and content are provided by thoughts and feelings prior to, posterior to, and outside of cessation itself.[21]

For Dōgen's part, he was vehemently critical of his contemporaries and predecessors in Buddhism who misrepresented meditation as "stopping thoughts, absorbed in quietude" (*sokuryo gyōjaku*) and who advocated "returning to the source, back to the origin" (*gengen hempon*).[22] Not-thinking is not a blank consciousness, nor the stoppage of thinking, nor a comatose state. From the perspective of the phenomenology of religion, this method of "dark sinking" (*konchin*) is fundamentally kindred to an age-old yogic-jhānic quest that Mircea Eliade calls "enstasis" (in contrast to ecstasy)—that is, the withdrawal from the external world by methodically purging the mind and consciousness of all content.[23] In terms of Eliade's useful concept, Dōgen struggled throughout his monastic career to overcome psychological, subjectivistic, and absorptionist tendencies and residues in Zen that were connected with the Buddhist enstasis.

Consider this alternative interpretation of not-thinking: That which is not/beyond comprehension is metaphycisized (epistemologically and/or ontologically) in such a way that it is viewed as the cosmic source, or as the highest or ultimate cognition.[24] In either case, thinking is dealt with as inferior and unreal, either to be supplanted by the really real or the absolutely true, or to be tolerated as a necessary evil for attaining a soteriological end.[25] For Dōgen, not-thinking is not a simple negation of thinking, in the sense of abandoning it for the sake of overcoming it. Dōgen was well aware of such a dualistic usage when he wrote:

> [The meaning of the ninety-day summer retreat is such that] thinking as discrimination cannot fathom it, nor can not-thinking as discrimination penetrate it. It is far beyond the reach of both thinking and not-thinking [as conceived in a dualism]."[26]

He clearly underscores the inadequacy of the dualistic conception. Instead Dōgen has this to say emphatically:

> You might think that the measure of the body-mind, because it *is* the measure of the body-mind, is far from being Dharma-nature, but such a thought is itself of Dharma-nature. You might also think that the measure of the body-mind, because it *is not* the measure of the body-mind, is not Dharma-nature, but this very thinking is itself of Dharma-nature as well. Thinking and not-thinking *alike* are of Dharma-nature.[27]

As I have already alluded to before, Dōgen's view is concerned not only with surmounting a dualism of thinking and not-thinking, but also with immersing oneself dialogically in their duality (without devaluating or minimizing their differences and tensions) as part and parcel of the soteric exploration. Without the latter, realization is not sufficient and efficacious enough. Thus Dōgen radicalizes his method.

For the sake of our understanding, let me formulate not-thinking in a different way: "That *thinking* which is not/beyond thinking." Note the difference from "*that which is* not/beyond thinking," which is prone to various dangers of metaphysicization that alienate thinking and not-thinking from one another in the salvific process. Dōgen's emphasis, in my view, lies not only in *not*-thinking but not-*thinking*; after all, not-thinking is conceivable only in view of thinking. Discontinuity and continuity between the two are hence better reflected in "that thinking which is not/beyond thinking." In Dōgen's view, therefore, thinking and not-thinking are the foci that accompany the third focus "nonthinking," also called "right thinking" (*shōshiyui*; *shōshiryō*). Not-thinking neither precedes nor succeeds, nor is outside or behind, thinking. There is no agent or consciousness behind not-thinking that thinks; in keeping with the notion of emptiness, not-thinking cannot and should not be reified. "We actualize thinking and not-thinking alike in and through emptiness," Dōgen writes.[28] For these reasons, not-thinking is coextensive and coeternal with thinking. Not-thinking *is* thinking, and vice versa.

The "not" in not-thinking is not a simple negation as in other ways in Dōgen's religion. Broadly speaking, the "not" informs thinking of its own fundamental limitations and possibilities to be fulfilled.[29] Although aware of its deficiencies and imperfections, thinking still possesses the trangressive impulse to break through the habitual, the orderly, the self-evident, the established, and the unjust, exploring and experimenting with its own abysmal depths, in terms of further possibilities, by penetrating even the marginal, the elusive, the forgotten, the forbidden, and the unknown. Though sometimes inordinately exaggerated, such a transgressive impulse has generated an iconoclastic, subversive streak in Zen.[30] For Dōgen's part, he neither psychologizes nor metaphysicizes not-thinking, but instead, treats it soteriologically in order for it to serve as a radical critique of thinking and as a window to new horizons of thinking. In short, not-thinking is neither the psychological nor the metaphysical ground of thinking, but is simply a focus—a conceptual construct. That said, not only are those functions of not-thinking *inherent* in thinking itself (according to the pan-Buddhist logic we are now familiar with), but are *intimate* with thinking (according to Dōgen's logic of intimacy). Intimacy does not signify a fusion of not-thinking and thinking, as in, say, the mystical "coincidence of opposites," nor does it mean a conglutination of them. Differences between them are alive, not obliterated, and still, the two soteric foci are intimate in their dialogical communion. Intimacy is a special relationship between the two foci that is *practiced* despite and/or because of their differences and tensions.

Along the same line of thought, Dōgen also presents his reading of "the mind as the unattainable" (*shin-fukatoku*). This notion in Zen was usually taken to mean that the mind is altogether beyond human comprehension and, as such, ultimately unknowable and unobtainable. The underlying assumption here was that the discriminative mind is bound to fail to know the unattainable. By contrast, Dōgen gives, not surprisingly, an existential thrust to the notion by saying that the mind is now construed as the workings of the very unattainable itself. Freed from metaphysical moorings as the object of cognition, the unattainable is an operative force in the practitioner's transformative process here and now.[31] The unattainable is "ever intimate" (*shinzō*) with, and transparent to, one's everyday mind and its activities. "Thoughts and discriminations of right this moment," Dōgen writes, "are none other than the mind as the unattainable."[32]

In this connection, it is noteworthy that Dōgen's mysticism of the unattainable is a far cry from apophatic mysticism, variations of which abound the world over, as in the ineffable in the negative theology of the West, the unnameable in Taoism, and *neti neti* ("not this, not that") in Upanishadic philosophy, to name just a few.[33] In those traditions, God, the Way, Brahman, and the like are said to be known by negating our language and thought systematically. The farther you retreat into the ineffable by the method of negation (via negativa), the nearer you are to the core of ultimate reality/truth. Ineffability/unnameability has to do with the nonlinguistic and nonconceptual cognition of ultimate reality/truth, for which human language and thought are totally unfit. Dōgen thinks otherwise: Ineffability is not due to thought's failure to describe reality; it is a lure of quest and adventure. It is in fact intrinsic to the temporality of all dharmas, so that it can be practiced in the daily life of practitioners, rather than being endlessly obsessed over and held in fascination by them. Ineffability is a designation for praxis in temporality.

Thought is thus "ever already" (*isō*) as ineffable, unnameable, and unattainable as reality. Thanks to the notion of emptiness, thought, as much as reality, is liberated from metaphysically as well as psychologically imposed referential constraints, so as to be able to practice ineffability/unnameability as unattainability in the soteric context. In brief, the bifurcation of reality and thought collapses, and a new relationship of intimacy is established between them for the sake of realization.

Related to Dōgen's usage of negatives are interrogatives such as *somo, shimo, nani, ka, tare* ("what," "how," "who," "which") that are frequently used in his writings as the affirmation of the mystery of existence. Although I have discussed the matter in some detail elsewhere,[34] let me cite just one example in the present context—Dōgen's reading of the sixth ancestor Ta-chien Hui-neng's question "What is this that comes thus?" (*shi shimo-butsu immorai*) that was addressed to Nan-yüeh Ta-hui (677–744):

> Regarding this saying, "thus(ness)" cannot be doubted, because it is beyond human comprehension [and incomprehension]. Because "this" [a particular thing] is "what," all things are always truly the what, and each and every thing is always truly the what. You should thoroughly investigate this. "What" is not a doubt; it is "thusness's coming."[35]

Hui-neng's "question" challenges Nan-yüeh to penetrate the salvific reality ("what") of his appearance before Ta-chien (as "thusness's coming"). As the

Zen saying goes, the answer is "ever already" within the question (*monjo no dōtoku*).[36] Just as the self is always questionable and problematic, so is the world we live in. Nevertheless, that very questionableness is a challenge and an opportunity for practitioners to discern and realize "what" as "thusness's coming." While living amid this mystery of the question and the answer, they must also continue to ask the rhetorical question "How is it necessarily so?" (*kahitsu*). This question always implies, and hence is often accompanied by, "Not necessarily" (*fuhitsu*).[37]

All in all, Dōgen conceives not-thinking to be less *"that which is* not/ beyond thinking" than "that *thinking* which is not/beyond thinking." He refuses to frame the issue in terms of thought and reality (or appearance and reality). Thinking and not-thinking as the two foci of zazen practice are dialectically related to each other. In this dynamic, thinking is not-thinking, not-thinking is thinking. In passing, thinking and not-thinking may be regarded as the rational and the nonrational, respectively; the irrational then results from misuse and abuse of the rational and the nonrational. Remember, however, that the rational, the nonrational, and the irrational are all under the aegis of nonthinking in Dōgen's Zen, to which we will now turn.

5

In light of the foregoing analysis, we can now better understand the dialogue between Yüeh-shan and the monastic, in particular, the Great Teacher's "[By way of] nonthinking." Dōgen's comment on this terse reply is: "The use of nonthinking is unmistakable, and yet, to think through not-thinking, we always exert nonthinking." He expressly asserts that nonthinking is for use and exertion (*shiyōsuru*; *mochiiru*) in the salvific endeavor. This is why he also calls nonthinking "the essential method" (*yōjutsu*) or "the dharmic method" (*hōjutsu*)—therefore by implication, as the practice—of seated meditation. Nonthinking is the essential method of zazen to be employed by the meditator. It is *praxis*, not *theoria, gnosis,* or *logos,* as many philosophically minded commentators of Dōgen's thought would have us believe.

Nonthinking is also identified by Dōgen as "right thinking" (*shōshiyui*; *shōshiryō*; *shōshi*), one of the categories in the eightfold right path (*hasshōdō*) that leads to the cessation of suffering and the attainment of *nirvāṇa*.[38] This hermeneutic move is noteworthy from the perspective of the eightfold right path—it implies that right thought is not only to be practiced *simultaneously* in conjunction with the seven other categories of the path (i.e., right understanding, right speech, right action, right livelihood, right effort, right mindfulness, and right concentration), but also is the *kernel* of them all, that is, of the Buddhist path to liberation. This is in itself quite a novel reinterpretation of the eightfold path as the early Buddhist teaching of praxis. (Needless to say, that thinking in this context involves not only cognitive qualities, such as conceptualization, reflection, deliberation, and criticism, but also affective and conative ones, such as feeling, emotion, volition, and desire.) Furthermore, in the context of the three divisions of the eightfold path—morality, meditation, and wisdom (*kai-jō-e*)—Dōgen singles out right thought from the division of wisdom. He takes it to be the essence of *meditation*, as if he were overriding the conventional arrangement of right effort, right mindfulness and right concentration under the division of meditation.[39] Is he endorsing the subitist (sudden enlightenment) advocacy of wisdom by rejecting meditation? Or is he thoroughly radicalizing meditation by framing it in this fashion? The whole picture is indeed extremely complex, and yet, my sense is that by lifting right thinking as the kernel of Buddhist praxis and equating it with nonthinking, Dōgen is not only challenging the conventional divisions of morality, meditation, and wisdom in Buddhism, but also grappling with the thorny problems of wisdom and meditation in Zen. (We shall return to this matter presently.)

What is *right* thinking in Dōgen's religion? First and foremost, right thinking is informed, purified, and empowered by the cardinal principle of emptiness, as signified by *non*thinking. Emptiness is not any ultimate reality or its attribute, nor is it concerned with the existence or nonexistence of ultimate reality; it is simply a salvific designation connoting the absence of any self-existent essence (*jishō*). Hence its function is to liberate practitioners so that they may freely and openly explore and experiment with soteric possibilities without being trammeled by substantialist, representational obsessions. Nonthinking, empowered now, may be likened to the "custodian" of emptiness in the dynamics of Zen realization. Such a function of nonthinking is what Dōgen seems to have had in mind by "someone" in his enigmatic statement: "There is 'someone' in nonthinking, and this someone sustains the one [who sits in zazen]." Or to put it differently, in Dōgen's schematic terms, nonthinking may be regarded as the "mediator" between thinking and not-thinking. By virtue of such nonthinking's custodial or mediatory function, the meditator's thinking (as well as not-thinking) is guarded against the pitfalls and dangers of a reifying, referential mindset. It is freed cognitively, affectively, and conatively to negotiate the Way, by wisely and compassionately dealing with the mundane matters in everyday life. As I have quoted before, Dōgen states:

"We actualize thinking and not-thinking alike in and through emptiness." We can now read it as: "We actualize thinking and not-thinking in and through nonthinking/right thinking." The point I wish to highlight is that right thinking for Dōgen has to do with not only the deconstructive role of emptiness, but the reconstructive one in the worldly arena. It goes beyond overcoming substantialism and attachment.

The issue of how to think authentically *must* concern itself with the nitty-gritty of the human situation—this aspect has been largely overlooked by commentators on nonthinking. More often than not, nonthinking is interpreted by some as something that neutralizes tensions between thinking and not-thinking by transcending their supposed impediments. But tensions are not just impediments. As the method of zazen, nonthinking orients thinking and not-thinking; it facilitates and negotiates ongoing dialogue between them, generating right thinking that is responsive to, and responsible for, daily affairs. Yet it is free and unattached to them. It goes without saying that Dōgen's disdain for hierarchical and teleological ways of treating nonthinking in relation to thinking and not-thinking is quite patent.

Thus, in view of what we have discussed in the preceding chapters, I now ask readers to recall the analogy of the steelyard, in which the function of emptiness is measuring the weight of an object in order to produce fairness in a transaction. In our complex human situation, the measuring activity must be a fine-tuned calibration in every aspect of our existence, especially in the area of reflective and critical thinking; the principle of fairness, in contrast, is ever dynamic and polysemous like "the shattered reflection of the moon." Be that as it may, Dōgen's notion of nonthinking points to the enormously complex and challenging task of practitioners to think through their personal as well as social needs, concerns, and problems in keeping with the cardinal principle of fairness.

Nonthinking, qua emptiness, is that "calibrator" which skillfully negotiates the interface between the act of calibration and the truth of fairness, both of which are, as foci, always complex in accordance with a given situation. This of course does not imply an opportunistic adaptation to existing conditions, but rather is principled and true to nature. At the same time, the authenticity of thinking defies assent to doctrines and dogmas, and conformity to rules and norms. Authenticity is open-ended, dynamic, and multidimensional, with innumerable forms. The corollary of this view is that there are countless variations on the theme of "the enlightened one" (*kakusha*). The one-dimensional, stereotypical image of the Zen personage cannot stand up to our critical analysis.

Non/right *thinking* is thus not only restored from its relegation and legitimized in the soteriological scheme of things, but has now become pivotal in Dōgen's vision of meditative practice. It is the new key to the understanding of praxis in his religion. Consider Dōgen's statement on the ocean-reflections *samādhi* (*kaiin zammai*), the meditative state of enlightenment Śākyamuni the Buddha is said to have entered before proclaiming the truth of the *Flower Ornament Sūtra* (*Kegon kyō*):

> All the buddha-ancestors are always what they are because of the ocean-reflections *samādhi*. As they float around in this samādhic [ocean], there is a time for discourse, a time for enlightenment, and a time for discipline. The [samādhic] ocean has power that is conducive to [the buddha-ancestors'] activities on its surface *and* along its deepest bottom. Such is [the import of Yüeh-shan Wei-yen's saying] "[For the time being,] I move along the floor of the deepest ocean," which means he moves [simultaneously] on the surface of the ocean.[40]

Figuratively referred to as the ocean, the *samādhi* reflects all things of the universe as they are on its calm, placid surface like images in a mirror. Elsewhere in the same "Kaiin zammai" fascicle (1242), Dōgen observes that the samādhic ocean *is* all existence. From this standpoint Dōgen holds that the ocean has the efficacious power to embrace and nurture movements both on its surface and in its depth. *Samādhi* is no longer a psychological, absorptionist, enstatic, or human-centered phenomenon.

It is worth noting in this connection that, at the beginning of the *Shōbōgenzō*, "Uji" (1240), Dōgen quotes Yüeh-shan Wei-yen's saying which reads in part: "For the time being, I stand on top of the highest mountain. For the time being, I move along the floor of the deepest ocean." We are now familiar with the fact that he transforms "for the time being" (*arutoki*) into "existence-time" (*uji*): Each and every existence is without exception a temporal being that is at once time bound and time free. Humans are such paradoxical beings. The top of the highest mountain and the bottom of the deepest ocean in the "Uji" is now modulated to the ocean surface and the ocean floor in the "Kaiin zammai." The point I wish to underscore for readers is that *samādhi* is radically temporalized in such a way that it embraces the surface and the bottom alike at this moment (*shōtō immoji*), regardless of where you are, and thus transforms itself into an anthropo-cosmic soteriological event.

This expansive (cosmicized beyond the anthropic orientation), yet existential (temporal) view of *samādhi* with its foci of "the surface of the ocean" and "the bottom of the ocean" is analogous to nonthinking with its foci of thinking and not-thinking. Just as thinking and not-thinking are nondually one in all authentic thinking, so are the surface and the bottom relative to the ocean-reflections *samādhi*. In the "Kaiin-zammai" fascicle, written in 1242 about a month after the "Zazenshin" fascicle, Dōgen strongly suggests rapport between *samādhi* and nonthinking. In fact, in Dōgen's Zen, *samādhi* is nonthinking, implying not only that it radically differs from a reductive psychological phenomenon, but also that there is an unabashed alliance between meditation and wisdom.

The term "nonthinking" appears in Dōgen's meditation manuals, most notably in his so-called popular text *Fukan zazengi* (A General Recommendation for the Principles of Zazen). Because of the importance of the latter text for the understanding of the evolution of Dōgen's thought on zazen, let me quickly summarize recent studies on this subject: (1) Immediately upon his return from China in 1227 (the third year of the Karoku era), Dōgen composed a manual of zazen, the Karoku text, which is now nonextant and is usually regarded as the urtext of the *Fukan zazengi*. (2) Later in 1233 (the first year of the Tempuku era), Dōgen made an autograph copy of the *Fukan zazengi*, known as the Tempuku text, which is the earliest extant *Fukan zazengi*. Although the Tempuku text is presumed by some as a fair copy of the Karoku text, the exact nature of the relationship between the Karoku and Tempuku texts cannot be determined. The former is nonextant, hence its contents are unknown to us. (3) Around 1243, Dōgen revised the Tempuku text, and therein produced the popular (or Kōroku) text to reflect his mature view of zazen that had developed in the years between these two recensions. (4) In view of the fact that, by his own account, Dōgen intended to compose a zazen manual based on and improving upon the *Tso-ch'an i*, an important meditation primer of the Northern Sung by Ch'ang-lu Tsung-tse (d. circa 1106), the Tempuku *Fukan zazengi* and the *Tso-ch'an i* are compared to one another, with notable disparities between the two. (5) Significant differences are also found between the Tempuku and popular versions of the *Fukan zazengi*. (6) These comparative studies clearly demonstrate that Dōgen endeavored, throughout his monastic career, to root out dhyānic (absorptionist), psychological (subjectivistic), and teleological implications and vestiges, and to finally declare nonthinking as the pivot of meditation. And (7) "nonthinking" also appears in Dōgen's other meditation manuals, all written in the same period as the popular text *Fukan zazengi*.[41]

In view of all this, nonthinking can be regarded as representing Dōgen's most mature view on meditation. A full understanding of the significance and implications of this methodological and hermeneutic maneuver during the period of 1242–1245 is yet to be made in Dōgen studies.[42]

6

As noted before, despite the fact that there is the official alliance of tranquility and insight in the Theravāda tradition, of calm and discernment in the T'ien-t'ai/Tendai school, and of meditation and wisdom in Ch'an/Zen, the precise nature of the relationship between tranquility/calm/meditation on the one hand, and insight/discernment/wisdom on the other, has by no means been clear in those traditions. In particular, Zen history is fraught with controversies surrounding this issue, as in subitism vs. gradualism, silent-illumination zen vs. kōan-introspection zen, and the like. What emerges clearly from the foregoing investigation is the fact that Dōgen's Zen cannot be pigeonholed by any traditional labels. He altogether defies such categorizations.

Fully cognizant of all the issues and problems involved, Dōgen critically examined zazen's scope, depth, and precision and completely reexpressed it in terms of nonthinking through thinking and not-thinking, with a thorough praxis orientation. In this reframed context, nonthinking is not so much that which transcends thinking and not-thinking epistemologically and/or ontologically. Rather, it is that which is firmly embedded in them as part and parcel of the temporal existence. From the perspective of expression (*dōtoku*), we now know that nonthinking is none other than that thinking which explicates the expressible, by way of the creative interaction between the already expressed and the not yet expressed/the inexpressible. The expressible in the salvific context is a clearer, more penetrating *discrimination*—in other words, a right discrimination. In this manner, thinking, hitherto ostracized as the foremost impediment to Zen realization, is now deemed as the pivotal practice of zazen itself. Gone is the fascination with the endless absorption in the undifferentiated. Instead, practitioners now practice right thinking to attain the authenticity of their practice.

Dōgen's insistence on the centrality of thinking in zazen by no means implies his wholesale dismissal of what we today call mystical/oceanic/peak experience. Note that his notion of thinking is grounded in that of the body-mind. By the same token, the thinking in question is a much more expansive notion that embraces mystical experience wholeheartedly. But Dōgen's overriding concern is with the issue of how practitioners can and ought to implement their religious or mystical experience in terms of the *worldly truth* of the revalorized situation. Accordingly, the examination of that experience by way of reflective, critical thinking is absolutely vital to their practice. To put it differently, Dōgen's method goes beyond traditionally exalted Zen virtues, such as those of silence and nonattachment.

Such a view of nonthinking might appear to us as strikingly similar to the view of some Buddhists, certainly Critical Buddhists, who grant wisdom/*prajñā* the privilege of having a higher and more ultimate soteriological status over meditation/*dhyāna*.[43] By treating nonthinking as the essence of zazen, is Dōgen in reality replacing meditation with wisdom? What is the precise nature of such a formulation of meditation? Such questions become not only plausible, but urgent, in view of the fact that as even Terada Tōru, hardly a Critical Buddhist himself, observes, the overall impression we get from the *Shōbōgenzō* is less Dōgen the meditator than Dōgen the thinker. Consequently, the Dōgen who single-mindedly engaged in zazen is virtually invisible.[44] Thus additional questions emerge: What are we to make of this discrepancy? Is Dōgen self-contradictory in this regard? Is there a rupture between Dōgen the meditator and Dōgen the thinker?

I wish to submit just two points regarding this matter: (1) While endeavoring to purge meditation of enstatic and subjectivistic residues, Dōgen never dismissed it qua meditation. For him, meditative experience should in itself have a legitimate place in the realizational process, not a second-rate status as compared with wisdom. When the meditator has, for example, an ineffable mystical experience, that episode of his/her life is "illumined," whereas all others—notably linguistic ones—are "darkened," in accordance with Dōgen's dictum "As one side is illumined, the other is darkened." The *in*effable, however self-evident it may be, does not imply the absence of linguistic mediations; to the contrary, it is *affirmed* as such precisely because of linguistic mediations. Without the latter, the affirmation of the ineffable is unthinkable and impossible to experience in the first place. For this reason, what is "illumined" in one's life demands respect; what is "darkened" should never be forgotten. The task for practitioners is one of clarification and seeing through, not removal. (2) In this hermeneutic context, nonthinking takes on a radical significance by challenging not only the traditional view of meditation, but that of wisdom, which has had a proclivity to overdraw itself in terms of satori, *prajñā*-intuition, Zen spirituality, and universal truth—all characterized as *sui generis* and *causa sui*. But as noted before, Dōgen reminds us of wisdom's intrinsic ambiguity. Indeed, it was anathema to Dōgen's way of thinking to privilege wisdom over meditation in a hierarchical, teleological framework. Thus, just as he raised Zen discourse on zazen and kōan to a new height, so he did with meditation and wisdom through his notion of nonthinking. As a pair of salvific foci, they inform and redeem each other.

CHAPTER 6

Radical Reason: *Dōri*

I

Nonthinking as a crucially important methodological and hermeneutic move in Dōgen's Zen has a number of further implications, especially in regard to what I wish to pursue in the present chapter, namely reason (*dōri*). In a preliminary fashion, let me illustrate just one example: On the one hand, from the standpoint of religious *experience*, this move implies that meditative experience (*jō; dhyāna*) is emancipated from its transic, anthropocentric, and teleological preoccupations of the mind. In contemporary terms it means freedom from "pure consciousness," "pure experience," "altered states of consciousness," and so forth. The subject matter is hotly debated today especially around meditation and mysticism in such fields as the philosophy of religion and transpersonal psychology.[1] For Dōgen's part, his Zen shifts attention from the simple interior state of the mind to all the realities of the self and universe—the anthropo-cosmic totality—that are precisely what he means by the "body-mind" (*shinjin*). In other words, meditation is not so much a retreat from the external world as it is an opening up of the body-mind to the mystery of the inner and outer world and beyond. Dōgen does not repudiate the experiential dimensions of meditation outright, but wants to liberate and restore them to the total, dynamic context of things as they are.

On the other hand, religious *thought* in Zen, often framed in terms of transcendent wisdom (*e; prajñā*), is also freed and empowered by way of nonthinking. It is now fully rooted in, and cognizant of, the intellectual and moral nitty-gritty of daily activities rather than divorced from it. Thoroughly temporalized, it is no longer fixated on its grandiose claim for universal, self-evident validity. Such a stance is a radical challenge to the exaltation of, and the overconfidence in, the mind—in contrast to the disparagement of the body. In the Western metaphysical tradition, "the secession of the logos," according to Martin Heidegger, started with Plato and Aristotle and culminated in Hegel, with a sharp dichotomy between thought and reality as well as with the hegemony of thought and reason over everything else.[2] (We are today still embroiled in the vortex of this radical critique of metaphysics—and of reason—that has overturned the very metaphysical foundation itself.) By contrast, Dōgen would have vehemently challenged such an alienated, disembodied, repressive notion of thought. Thus, in his Zen, both experience and thought are at once deconstructed and reconstructed through nonthinking; they are therefore free from bifurcation without compromising their differences and tensions.

Now, the workings of nonthinking are in essence those of emptiness within temporality. At this point I call attention again to the supreme importance of temporality, which profoundly shaped Dōgen's view of emptiness. I mention this at the outset of the present chapter because his deep concern with reason is ultimately embedded in what he calls "temporal conditions" (*jisetsu innen*)—the personal, historical, and cultural conditions of existence, as well as "vast and giddy karmic consciousness" (*gosshiki bōbō; bōbō gosshiki*) and "entwined vines" (*kattō*), that is, emotional, intellectual, and moral entanglements. "Understanding life lucidly and penetrating death thoroughly" (*ryōshō tasshi*), declares Dōgen, is accomplished by "just discerning the temporal conditions" (*tōkan jisetsu innen*); furthermore, "the temporal conditions can only be discerned through the temporal conditions themselves." This point is vitally important because Dōgen's sense of reason originates from and is nurtured by such a sensibility and commitment to temporality and existentiality. There is no tinge whatsoever in him of speculative or scholastic fascinations.

In this chapter, I shall pursue the problem of reason still further along this line of thought, specifically with respect to *dōri* (or *kotowari*), one of Dōgen's most favorite concepts, that connotes "truth," "reason," "reasonableness," "justice," "naturalness," and so on. Broadly speaking, our concern has to do with reason and rationality in Dōgen's soteriology, which has been grossly neglected in Dōgen studies. We may ask, why should we bother with the subject in the first place when the issue is in such disrepute in this day and age of postmodernism? Hasn't the hitherto undisputed hegemony of the Enlightenment and scientific rationalism been relentlessly challenged? In such a contemporary cultural milieu, aren't we already all too familiar with Zen's unconventional, irreverent, iconographic temperament that "goes against the grain" of practically every possible cultural habit and trait? And, not surprisingly, has not comparability between Zen and postmodernism been widely explored by a number of philosophers?[3]

All these questions are well taken. Yet, whatever the merits and demerits of postmodernism may be, I am deeply convinced more than ever that no age in human history calls for the genuine understanding and re-vision of reason more urgently than ours. In any event, as shown in the previous chapters, and as more will follow presently, Dōgen's quest for reason evolved concurrently with his quest for authentic practice.

2

The word *dōri* consists of two Chinese characters: *Dō* (*tao*) and *ri* (*li*). The *dō* means "a road," "a path," or "a way," on which you tread, walk, and travel; from this it is commonly translated as "the Way" when employed in Chinese and other East Asian religious and philosophical traditions. The Way signifies wide-ranging meanings such as proper human conduct, social organizations, and the processes of the phenomenal world, as well as the discernible order and unnameable mystery of the universe—all of this strongly emphasizes the proper course of action by humans.[4] It is noteworthy that the notion of *dō* in the East Asian traditions has a single common thread, namely, the meaning of walking, journeying, or movement along a path. The Way is never extricated from the processes of phenomena themselves. As such, it is neither a metaphysical principle, nor a moral law external to phenomena, nor a fate dictated from without, nor a God of absolute transcendence. As Helmut Wilhelm observes, the meaning of the Way is "not grasped in stasis but in movement." Hence: "The meaning consists of the Way (Tao) of change and it can be understood only by treading this Way. In this world of change, meaning appears in grasping and pursuing, in treading the Way, in acting out the meaning."[5]

In line with such a worldview, the *dō* in East Asian Buddhism is closely associated with specifically Buddhist practices as precepts, rules, and disciplines. *Dō* is adopted to signify *mārga* or *pratipat*, a path of religious precepts and disciplines which one follows in order to attain liberation, as in *hasshōdō* ("the eightfold path"), *chūdō* ("the middle way"), *rokudō* ("the six destinies") in which sentient beings are reborn according to their karmic consequences, and *dōshin* ("the thought of enlightenment"). In contrast to the cognate word *hō* (*dharma*; *fa*), meaning "law," "truth," and "teaching," *dō* strongly connotes the praxis orientation. In this latter context we should remember that *dō* also means "to speak"; in relation to this, Dōgen provided deep insights into language in Zen praxis, as we saw in chapter 4.

The *ri* (*li*) is equally complex in its signification as used in East Asian culture. Roger T. Ames's analysis of *li* in the classical Confucian context is highly instructive for our purpose because he attempts to reconstruct the scope and depth of *li* by unraveling some meanings hitherto obscured by the most frequently adopted translations of *li*, such as "reason" and "principle."[6] In its classical usage, *li* signifies "order," "pattern," and "markings," and also the verbal functions of "to order," "to pattern," and "to mark." Following the lines of thought advanced by the distinction between the logical (or rational) order and the aesthetic order, which was offered by David L. Hall and Ames in their work,[7] Ames highlights some salient features of *li*: (1) The Chinese do not dichotomize between nature and culture in speaking of coherence or intelligibility; both nature and culture are embedded within the notion of *tao,* and hence are integral to *li.* (2) *Li* as the fabric of order is immanent in and emergent from the dynamic process of experience, which is neither exclusively subjective nor exclusively objective. (3) *Li* connotes both the uniqueness of each particular and the continuity that exists among all particulars; accordingly, it is both a unity and a multiplicity. (4) *Li* is understood to be the patterns of correlation, not Platonic *eidos* or any such essentialistic, metaphysically privileged variants. (5) *Li* is not restricted to human consciousness, does not bifurcate the animate and inanimate, agency and act, the intelligible and the sensible, and is contingent upon the ongoing process specific to natural, personal, social, and cultural conditions. (6) *Li* implies both description and norm, "is" and "ought." The "ought" here, however, does not suggest some teleological design or ideal order beyond and independent of historical and cultural existence. And finally, (7) *Li* involves both the cognitive and the affective (emotions and passions), and both epistemology (knowing) and ethics (authentic personhood).

All things considered, the *li* constitutes those patterns, rhythms, and regularities which humans discern as meaningful in carrying out their day-to-day activities, by participating in the dynamics of the natural, and according to their personal, historical, and cultural conditions and forces. Rationality is never regarded as an immutable, self-contained truth or essence transcendentally existent in a hierarchical, teleological world order, but is grasped in an ever-shifting process of human affairs in relation to nature, history, and culture.

Considered in the Buddhist context, *li*, like *tao*, attains enormous complexity in its signification: The word is employed to denote *siddhānta* ("fundamental principle/law") and, hence such Buddhist notions as thusness, emptiness, and equality, with a tendency to be associated with abstraction and speculation. It is combined with other words as in *rinyū* ("entry by the truth"), *ri-busshō* ("intrinsic Buddha-nature"), *ri-hosshin* ("the dharma-body as ultimate principle"), and so on. On the other hand, *li* is also used to signify, for example, *pramāha* ("to arrange," "to regulate," "to rectify"). It is particularly noteworthy that in Hua-yen thought *li* ("principle") is paired with *shih* ("phenomenon"), and their relationship is conceived in such a way that "the nonobstruction of *li* and *shih*" (*li-shih wu-ai*; *riji muge*) is further refined as "the nonobstruction of *shih* and *shih*" (*shih-shih wu-ai*; *jiji muge*)—in other words, the interpenetration and harmony of all phenomena. This shift in thinking is notable in that, while in India the relationship between the universal and the particular was the paramount concern, the Chinese tradition reconceptualized the whole problem in terms of relationship between one particular event and another and, by extension, among all events.[8] We glimpse here an aspect of the Sinicization of Buddhism and, for that matter, the continuity between classical Confucianism and Hua-yen thought.

The notion of *dōri* appeared in China as the Sino-Buddhist translation of the Sanskrit word *yukti* ("laws," "norms"), and yet as the compound word of *dō* and *ri*, it evolved in a close relationship with the immensely rich religio-philosophical traditions in China and other East Asian countries. Dōgen's view on *dōri* owed to this legacy enormously. Although I translate it as "reason" and occasionally as "reasonableness" in the present work for the sake of expediency, it brims with multiple meanings and sentiments far too fertile to be reduced to a one-dimensional conception of rationality that is all too familiar in our predominant Western culture.

Thus, to clear the way for our subsequent investigation, let me broadly outline a few essential observations: *Dōri* is broad and flexible enough in its capacity to embrace *logos, mythos, ethos,* and *pathos*; cognition, affection, and conation; nature and culture; fact and value; *theoria and praxis*; the self and the universe. Its boundary is open-ended and provisional, functioning always in and through human needs and interests, and yet is able to surpass its own limitations. What is more, *dōri* is practically oriented, enabling humans to participate in its countless configurations, rhythms, and regularities in life and the world as they discern meaningful. While fully engaged in discerning and enacting, *dōri* regulates, arranges, and manages, as much as it challenges, surmounts, and subverts.

3

Given the fact that the word *dōri* was popularly used in medieval Japan with a great variety of meanings—not only its usual ones such as truth, reason, reasonableness, morality, and naturalness, but others ranging from mores to the sense of impermanence to the inscrutable will of supernatural forces,[9] it may not be so surprising to see Dōgen's fondness of the word. He was altogether medieval in this regard. Some examples that illustrate his usage are "the reason of the skin, flesh, bones, and marrow entwining with each other like vines" (*hiniku kotsuzui no kattō suru dōri*), "the reason that one's self is temporal" (*jiko no toki naru dōri*), "the reason of total exertion" (*gūjin no dōri*), "the reason of total surrender" (*ninnin no dōri*), "the reason of words and letters" (*monji no dōri*), "the reason of the Buddha-dharma" (*buppō no dōri*), "the reason of arising and perishing from moment to moment" (*setsuna shōmetsu no dōri*), "the reason of karmic retribution" (*goppō no dōri*), and "the reason of cause and effect" (*inga no dōri*). Dōgen's usage, like his contemporaries in medieval Japan, included whatever norms, values, meanings, and mores were deemed to be reasonable, true, fair, virtuous, and natural in guiding one's thoughts and conduct.

Reason for Dōgen is located within his vision of an anthropo-cosmic situation that is thoroughly temporal and best described, as we now know, in terms of "entwined vines," "the vast and giddy karmic consciousness," and the like. It refuses to transcendentalize itself above and beyond that situation. Within this context, it does not posit itself in opposition to passion, unreason, or faith. It is not torn between the theoretical and practical, the pure and impure, or the spiritual and material. The task of reason is to understand, negotiate, configure, and clarify the forces, conditions, and problems of the ever-shifting situation, thereby orienting and guiding practitioners in their soteric enterprise. In other words, reason is not something in the abstract, but concrete and active, as a methodological and hermeneutic tool. As such, Dōgen regards reason as practice.

At the assembly of Abbot Ch'ang-sha Ching-ts'en [854–932], Minister Chu [n.d.] asked: "An earthworm is cut in two pieces; the two pieces are both moving. In which piece do you think Buddha-nature exists?" The teacher said: "Don't be deluded!" The minister replied: "But how do you explain their movement?" The teacher said: "Wind and fire are not dispersed."

In the minister's statement "An earthworm is cut in two pieces," is he assuming that it was just one piece prior to its being cut in two? In the buddha-ancestors' way of thinking, this cannot be the case. The earthworm is neither one piece from the beginning nor two as a result of being cut. Such expressions as "one" and "two" should be thoroughly investigated through practice.

Does the "two pieces" in "the two pieces are both moving" imply that there was a single piece before the cutting? Does it construe that single piece as something which transcends the Buddha? Whether or not the minister understood it does not matter, but the utterance "two pieces" itself should never be dismissed. Does it mean that while the divided two pieces were [originally] one entity, there is another entity besides? Speaking of their movement, [the minister] says, "both moving," but he should understand this in the sense that meditation, which moves [the passions], and wisdom, which removes [them], are altogether moving.

"In which piece do you think Buddha-nature exists?" This question should be rephrased as "Buddha-nature is cut in two pieces. In which piece do you think the earthworm exists?" You must examine this expression with great care. "The two pieces are both moving. In which piece does Buddha-nature exist?" Does it mean that because both are moving, [the movement] is not fit for Buddha-nature's abode? Or that even though both are moving, and hence move alike, Buddha-nature's abode must be in either one of them?

The teacher said, "Don't be deluded!" What is its fundamental meaning? He speaks of having no *delusory thought*. Therefore, you should thoroughly study the following various questions: Does he mean that there is no delusory thought in the movement of the two pieces, and that it is, as such, not delusory thought? Is he simply saying that Buddha-nature is free of delusory thought? Or, is he trying to say that beyond the arguments in terms of Buddha-nature and the two pieces, there is no delusion whatsoever?

"But how do you explain their movement?" Does it mean that since [the two pieces] are moving, another Buddha-nature should be added [to the original one]? Or does it mean that since they are moving, they are not Buddha-nature?

"Wind and fire are not dispersed"—this utterance should bring out Buddha-nature here. Should we construe [the movement of the earthworm-in-two-pieces] as Buddha-nature? Or, as wind and fire? We must not say that Buddha-nature and wind and fire appear simultaneously, or that one appears, while the other does not, or that wind and fire per se are Buddha-nature. For this reason, Ch'ang-sha does not say the earthworm has Buddha-nature or that it has no Buddha-nature; he just says: "Don't be deluded!" and "Wind and fire are not dispersed." The workings of Buddha-nature should be understood through Ch'ang-sha's sayings. You should quietly investigate the words, "Wind and fire are not dispersed." What meaning is there in "not dispersed"? Does it signify the situation in which wind and fire are brought together, but the time for them to be dispersed has not yet arrived? Such a notion cannot be the case. "Wind and fire are not dispersed" is the Buddha expounding the Dharma; "not dispersed are wind and fire" is the Dharma expounding the Buddha. For example, it is the arrival of the occasion that expounds the Dharma of a single sound; it is the occasion of the arrival that is the single sound expounding the Dharma. The Dharma is the single sound, because it is the single-sound Dharma.[10]

This passage obviously has to do with the existence and nonexistence of Buddha-nature in relation to the two moving pieces of an earthworm. However, my purpose here is to focus on Dōgen's view of reason. For lack of space, I shall state three points summarily:

1. The foregoing passage demonstrates Dōgen's analytic and critical thinking in search of clarity and depth of meaning. In fact, I consider this as a very good example of his *practice*. He deeply probes the kōan at hand, asking himself as well as readers/audience seemingly endless questions that dissect the problem from every possible angle—of existing and/or not existing, moving and/or not moving, one and/or two, before and/or after, delusion and/or no delusion, dispersed and/or not dispersed—all revolving around the *workings* of Buddha-nature, by way of effectively employing the dynamic, dialectical relationship between duality and nonduality. For our purpose at the moment, the tenacity of Dōgen's critical analysis is noteworthy. Thus, instead of exhorting others to adopt a ready-made notion of Buddha-nature, Dōgen challenges them to examine and elucidate it critically and unremittingly. Without such efforts, no clarity and depth of dharmas—things, thoughts, imagination—can be attained. Reason is *not* extra-, trans-, pre-, or postdharmic. Reason's entwined vines are comprised by countless forces and conditions of the self and world—reasons, causes, motives, excuses, purposes, meanings, values, explanations, and so forth. They are coextensive and coeternal with Buddha-nature.[11]

2. "Don't be deluded!" (*makumōzō*) in Zen is all too often employed solely in the sense of discouraging or rejecting dualistic thought, but Dōgen's questions clearly suggest his appreciation of thinking that is, as such, neither delusory or not delusory. "Don't be deluded!" therefore implies: "Don't be deluded by the tricks/snares of language, thinking and reason." Remember what we discussed in chapter 1 regarding delusion and enlightenment. Dōgen never loses sight of the dark side of *delusory* reason. Even so, if Nietzsche reminds us of reason as "the slave of the passions," Dōgen shows us that reason is also the bearer of realization despite its all-too-human limitations.

3. Ch'ang-sha's terse answer "Wind and fire are not dispersed" repudiates, once and for all, any facile explanation as the one that hypothesizes the metaphysical source from which wind and fire—which together with earth and water make up the four elements—originate and to which they return. Zen soteriology has nothing to do with any kind of explanation or speculation. Instead, it boils down to *that* "Wind and fire are not dispersed"—a vision of the conditioned existence. The practitioner's task then is to elucidate and penetrate it through reason, rather than to seek

the why, the how, or the when. This is why Ch'ang-sha was noncommittal in answering whether "an earthworm has Buddha-nature" or "an earthworm has no Buddha-nature." Existence and nonexistence do not apply to Buddha-nature. This incommensurability, however, should not be overstated. Dōgen, in fact, discusses "the Buddha-nature of existence" (*u-busshō*) and "the Buddha-nature of nonexistence" (*mu-busshō*) in the "Busshō" fascicle (1241), but they are employed strictly for his praxis orientation. This hermeneutic move shows that Buddha-nature excludes nothing from its purview. Yet, the locus of all this is found in the *conditioned existence*, only in which are the workings of Buddha-nature and of reason meaningful.[12] It is "the single-sound Dharma."

4

Dōgen refers to reason as "evident and impartial" (*rekinen to shite watakushi nashi*), as in the case of the reason of (moral) causation.[13] He also refers to it as "imperative" (*hitsuzen naru*), as in the case of one's obligation to repay the buddha-ancestors for their benevolence.[14] This characterization of reason can be properly appreciated in view of the fact that Dōgen rejects a fatalistic reading of karma and human nature, thereby insisting that humans, regardless of their past lives and present circumstances, are capable of and prepared for understanding and acting upon their predicament, however dark it may be. The senses of reasonableness, of fairness, of right and wrong, and the like, are absolutely required for the soteric scheme of things.

To Dōgen, the notion of karma was less a way of explaining an individual's lot in the present life based on actions in his/her previous lives than a way of assuring moral freedom and responsibility for the person to carve out his/her own destiny. The same holds true of Dōgen's way of appropriating the notion of "karmic retribution in the three stages of time" (*sanjigō*)—the maturation of karmic consequences in the present life, in the next life, and in the future lives after the next.[15] In this manner the twin concepts of karma and rebirth function as catalysts for the *present* in Dōgen's praxis-oriented religion.

The word *akiramu* has precisely such connotations: It involves seeing things clearly as they are in a given situation, discerning the possibilities and limitations of what one can and cannot do in terms of one's moral choice and action, and realizing what to relinquish and accept. In any responsible moral economy, these aspects of *akiramu*—discernment, relinquishment, and acceptance—go hand in hand. *Akiramu*, however, is also vulgarized in the common fatalistic parlance as meaning "to give up," "to resign oneself to," and "to accept one's fate," with no discernment, or relinquishment, or acceptance, in the genuine, critical sense. It goes without saying that such a diction is unacceptable in Dōgen's Zen.

Cause and effect in the moral sphere are now construed as the "perfected cause, fulfilled effect" (*en'in kaman*)—the contemporaneity (or nonduality) of cause and effect in realization.[16] As far as you live in the realm of causation, there is no escape from its inexorable law; this is called "not obscuring causation" (*fumai inga*). Nevertheless, when your thought, speech, and action are perfected in the present, their effects are "ever already" fulfilled in that very moment. The qualities of your being and action at this very moment matter most. Consequently, you are free amid the inexorable law; this is called "not falling into causation" (*furaku inga*). Thus, the reason of causation embraces both "not obscuring" and "not falling into" causation. At the interface of these two foci, reason is able to engage most rigorously with karmic causation.

The same tenor is also presented in his commentary on "Hymn for the Seven Past Buddhas' Precepts" (*shichibutsu tsūkaige*), which reads:

Not to commit any evil,
To do everything good,
And to purify one's mind,
This is the teaching of all the buddhas.[17]

And Dōgen's exposition:

When you are taught or teach about enlightenment in terms of concrete expression, it is heard as this ["not to commit any evil"]. Such is the case because it is the definitive expression of supreme enlightenment. It is unequivocally enlightenment's own words; accordingly, it speaks of enlightenment itself. Supreme enlightenment becomes words and is heard, whereby one vows "not to commit any evil" and diligently practices "not to commit any evil."[18]

As is evident from the above statement, Dōgen's moral reason refuses the conventional bifurcation of "is" and "ought," or of morality and religion. "Not to commit any evil" is "ever intimate" with the dialectical dynamics of practice and enlightenment. He goes so far as to say:

As we investigate the matter in this way, it becomes clear to us that "all evil" has all along had to do with [whether or not we exert the vow of] "not to

commit." Encouraged by such realization, we penetratingly see [the meaning of] "not to commit any evil" and, thereby, sit in meditation through and
through. . . . Consequently, evil does not arise from causes and conditions
[in abstractions], but depends solely on [whether or not we exert the vow
of] "not to commit"; evil does not perish by causes and conditions [in ab-
stractions], but depends solely on [whether or not we exert the vow of] "not
to commit." . . . Pitiful are those who see that evil is produced by various
causes and conditions, but who fail to see that these causes and conditions
intrinsically possess [the power of] "not to commit."[19]

Instead of engaging in a metaphysicization of evil or a theodicy of divine
justice, Dōgen insists that evil, whether it arises or perishes, is never extra-
neous to practitioners' moral purview—this is the power of the vow "not
to commit any evil." Furthermore, the causes and conditions in question
are not just causes and conditions in the theoretical sense, but possess the
intrinsic power to overcome evil, in and through practitioners' endeavors.
Thus, just as "the vast and giddy karmic consciousness" bears upon not
only human beings but all beings/things in the universe, so does the vow
of "not to commit any evil." This is Dōgen's *moral vision* of the universe. I
hasten to add that this is altogether alien to a moralization of the universe
as a worldview.

5

Reason is also related to *jinen* ("naturalness"), especially *hōni dōri*
(*dharmatā-yukti*), reason as "things as they are" or "the true nature of
things." This particular mode of reason is crucially important for understanding Dōgen, because naturalness, the true nature of things, and reason
are inseparably intertwined in the medieval Japanese Buddhist ethos in
general and in Tendai *hongaku* thought in particular.[20] In line with the latter, the notion of reason as the true nature of things, by and large, advocated
that state of spiritual freedom which transcended the law of dependent
origination (*engi*), and thus rejected cause and effect, arising and perishing,
and other cognate notions.

One of the most celebrated interpretations of the notion of *jinen* in
the history of Japanese Buddhism is of course Shinran's *jinen hōni* ("naturalness"). In his Pure Land thought, it signifies the workings of Amida
Buddha's original vow-power alone that allows no room whatsoever for
the practitioner's self-centered, calculative contrivance or for human efforts (*hakarai*). Moreover, in the dynamics of naturalness, "dharma-body

as suchness" (*shinnyo hosshin*), namely, the formless true reality, gives rise of itself to "dharma-body as compassionate means" (*hōben hosshin*), in other words Amida's saving activity, free of any design or calculation. Natural-ness thus encompasses the formless as well as its salvific dynamicity. In this manner, Shinran radically transformed the abstract universalism of *hōni dōri* into *jinen hōni*, an intensely existential and religious celebration of Amida's sole grace.[21]

As for Dōgen, he shared such an "other-power" (*tariki*) sensibility with Shinran. Consider "the reason of total surrender" (*ninnin no dōri*):

> The great Way of understanding life lucidly and penetrating death thor-oughly, as is unequivocally clear, [further] has a time-honored adage: "The great sage surrenders birth-and-death to the mind, surrenders birth-and-death to the body, surrenders birth-and-death to the Way, and surrenders birth-and-death to birth-and-death.[22]

The following statement is also strikingly similar to Shinran's religion:

> This birth-and-death itself is the life of the Buddha. . . . When you neither loathe nor crave it, only then do you enter the heart of the Buddha for the first time. But do not calculate it with your mind or explain it in words. When you cast off and forget your body and mind and plunge into the abode of the Buddha, so that the Buddha may act upon you and you may devote yourself completely to him, you become a buddha, liberated from the suf-fering of birth-and-death, without effort and anxiety.[23]

Devotional and pious qualities are unmistakably present in these utterances. Feelings and emotions possess their own reasons. Note that in Dōgen's Zen, devotion and wisdom, faith and enlightenment, and self-power and other-power, though often dichotomized by some Zen Buddhists, sustain and inform one another.

And yet, Dōgen rejects the notion of naturalness in the sense of spontaneous generation of things without the workings of causes and con-ditions, which amounts to a flat disavowal of moral endeavors. On this ac-count he vehemently attacks the "naturalist heresy" (*jinen gedō; tennen gedō*), and links such a view to Taoism, particularly Lao-tzu's and Chuang-tzu's thought.[24] For example, he takes on Chuang-tzu's statement, "The high and low, pain and pleasure, right and wrong, gain and loss—all these are natural," criticizing his failure to see the fact that they all result from moral causation, far from being naturally (causelessly) given.[25] Dōgen seems to draw upon the general Buddhist critique (prevalent in China since the sixth century) of the Taoist view of nature/naturalness (*tzu-jan*) as counter to the Buddhist doctrine of dependent origination. The seemingly *natural* way of things is, in the final analysis, the product of striving, not only in human terms but also in cosmic terms, as expressed, for instance, as "that practice-enlightenment which is exerted before the kalpa of nothingness" (*kūgō izen no shushō*) and "that kōan which is realized before the origin of the universe" (*chinchō izen no kōan*).[26] "To study the Buddha-dharma," declares Dōgen, "one should, first and foremost, understand causation clearly."[27]

It is notable that Dōgen prefers to use, instead of the adverbial form *jinen ni*, the other alternative words *onozukara* and *onorezukara*—adverbs with such meanings as "naturally," "effortlessly," "spontaneously," and "genuinely." When he must use *jinen ni* at all, he is quick to guard readers against the misleading connotations of the word:

> The high ancestor [Bodhidharma] said: "A flower opens its five petals and comes to fruition naturally." You should study the occasion of this flower's opening as well as its radiant light, color, and form. What a flower enfolds are its five petals; what the five petals unfold is the flower. The truth of "a flower" is declared in [Bodhidharma's saying]: "I first came to this land [China], transmitted the Dharma, and saved deluded beings"; the investigation of "[a flower's] light and color" lies in the study of this saying. "Coming to fruition" means what you make as a result of leaving it in your own hands: This is [the meaning of] "coming to fruition *naturally*." "Coming to fruition *naturally*" means cultivating cause and engendering effect. There are causes that are universally evident, there are also effects that are universally evident. In cultivating that causation which is universally evident, you engender that causation which is universally evident.[28]

The naturalness of the fruit-bearing in question is *cultivated* not automatic, and *engendered* not given, precisely due to the sense of reason that is heavily couched in the praxis orientation of karmic causation. There is no effortless-ness without effort. Spirituality devoid of intellectual and ethical endeavors is incomplete and, hence, unreasonable, as far as Dōgen is concerned. Furthermore, the reason of such karmic causation governs humanity and nature alike.

As is clear from the foregoing, Dōgen's paramount concern in his rejection of naturalism is, quite understandably, its devastating ethical, intellectual, and religious implications. Compared with Shinran's advocacy of the spontaneous unfolding of Amida's original vow-power, which tends to obscure practitioners' moral responsibility (and even capacity to respond morally) by transcendentalizing reason in the name of naturalness, Dōgen expressly declares that enlightenment *entails* morality, for the former collapses without the latter, and only in that light is the latter authenticated.

6

Dōgen presents his view of reason by way of treating Dharma-nature (*hosshō; dharmatā*), which he prefers to *hōni* (*dharmatā*), closely associated with *jinen* ("naturalness") and *hōnen* ("naturalness"), and for which he wrote the *Shōbōgenzō,* "Hosshō" fascicle (1243). The term "Dharma-nature" in Dōgen is almost synonymously used with such cognates as Buddha-nature (*busshō*), thusness (*shinnyo*), the true nature of all things (*shohō jissō*), and so on. Yet the word *dharma* becomes particularly pertinent in the present context by virtue of its multifaceted meanings in Buddhism—cosmic order and law, the Buddha's teaching, Buddhist truth and its practice, rules and norms of conduct, justice and righteousness, the ultimate constituents of reality (in this sense, "dharmas" in the plural is used), and by extension, all things/phenomena. Ranging in meaning from the ultimate to the worldly, its semantic proteanism is quite fitting for Dōgen's conception of reason and reasonableness. *Dōri* is not constrained by a particular boundary or horizon, nor by any particular faculty of the mind. Instead, it is a firefighter, so to speak, who applies his or her whole being to putting out a blazing fire. Reason in Dōgen's religion is mobilized in such an exigent salvific project by negotiating the Way multidimensionally.

Be that as it may, in the history of Buddhist thought, the Dharma is commonly regarded as antecedent to the historical Buddha who was just one of its manifestations; the buddhas may come and go but the Dharma is eternal. From this it is not too difficult to see why Dharma-nature was metaphysically privileged over dharmas. It may be construed as the first principle that instantiates all dharmas as its instances, or as the primordial source from which all dharmas issue and to which they all return, or as the ground of being by virtue of which dharmas are what they are. In short, Dharma-nature is not only metaphysicized but metaphysically privileged all too facilely as self-sufficient and self-caused (uncaused or spontaneously arising), therein robbing it of its genuinely dynamic *relationship* with dharmas. Dharma-nature and all things are alienated from each other and, as a result, are incapacitated as salvific symbols. This is what Dōgen calls "the bondage of Dharma-nature" (*hosshō no baku*); it is clearly against his sense of "the reason of Dharma-nautre" (*hosshō no dōri*).

For his part, Dōgen meticulously maneuvers his strategy of reason as the catalyst of relationality between Dharma-nature and all dharmas, without reifying either. The ultimate is not relativized; the relative is not absolutized. They are neither identical nor different in the dynamics of their dialectical, nondual interpenetration.

I would like to quote a few key passages regarding Dharma-nature:

[Some of those who pride themselves on having studied Buddhism for a number of years think] the way Dharma-nature is, is such that only after the triple world and the ten directions, which we now observe and experience, have been dissolved, will Dharma-nature manifest itself for the first time. They mistakenly reason that this Dharma-nature is not the universe now existing. The truth of Dharma-nature, however, should not follow such a view. [The relationship between] the universe and Dharma-nature [is so ever intimate that it] transcends a theory of identity and difference or an explanation in terms of oneness and separation. It is not the past, present and future, not extinction and permanence, not matter, feeling, perception, volition and consciousness. That is why Dharma-nature is what it is.[29]

Therefore, this here-now is none other than Dharma-nature; Dharma-nature is none other than this here-now. Wearing clothes and eating meals is the *samādhi* of Dharma-nature that wears clothes and eats meals. Realized is Dharma-nature as the clothes; realized is Dharma-nature as the meals; realized is Dharma-nature as the act of eating; and realized is Dharma-nature as the act of wearing. Apart from wearing clothes and eating meals, and apart from exchanging conversations, employing the six sense organs, and engaging in all kinds of everyday activities, your life is not of the *samādhi* of Dharma-nature, nor have you entered Dharma-nature.[30]

From the perspective of Dōgen's mysticism of intimacy in which reason is located, Dharma-nature and the phenomenal world cannot be reduced to opposites or polarities—such as identity and difference, and the one and the many, in the classical metaphysical sense. Rather, as I have suggested in the present work, they are best considered as soteriological foci, that is, relational constructs that guide, facilitate, and catalyze the realizational process.

Dōgen touches more specifically on Dharma-nature in connection with thinking and reason:

Days and months of countless kalpas constitute the temporal passage of Dharma-nature. The same holds true of the present and the future. To think that the measure of the body-mind is *nothing but* the measure of the body-mind, and that it is therefore alien from Dharma-nature—such thinking is itself none other than Dharma-nature. To think that the measure of the body-mind is *simply not* the measure of the body-mind, and that it is thus not Dharma-nature—such thinking is itself none other than Dharma-nature as well. [Therefore], thinking and not-thinking are both Dharma-nature. It is un-Buddhist to think that, insofar as [Dharma-]nature is concerned, water can neither flow nor circulate, and trees can neither grow nor wither.[31]

Śākyamuni the Buddha once said: "Thusness's form, thusness's nature." For this reason, flowers' blooming and leaves' falling are all thusness's nature. And yet, the foolish think that there should be no flowers' blooming, no leaves' falling in the realm of Dharma-nature. Just for a moment, instead of addressing your questions to other people, assume your questions to be your own assertions, or imagine them to be others' explanations. Then examine them penetratingly, time after time, and you will be free from [doubt]. Their hitherto-held thinking is not a wrong one so much as it is just the thinking they had when they failed to see [the reason of Dharma-nature] clearly. At the moment of seeing [the reason of Dharma-nature] clearly, you do *not erase* your [old] thinking. Flowers' blooming and leaves' falling are of themselves flowers' blooming and leaves' falling. The thinking that thinks there should be no flowers' blooming and no leaves' falling in the realm of Dharma-nature is in itself none other than Dharma-nature. It is that thinking in which you assumed your questions to be your own assertions that is now cast off. Accordingly, Dharma-nature as thusness *thinks*; thinking as Dharma-nature thinks *totally*. Such is the countenance [of total thinking].[32]

In these passages, Dōgen gives hermeneutic weight to the reason of Dharma-nature in relation to thinking (*shiryō*) and seeing clearly (*akiramu*). "Their hitherto held thinking is not a wrong one so much as it is just the thinking they had when they failed to see [the reason of Dharma-nature] clearly," says Dōgen. "At the moment of seeing [the reason of Dharma-nature] clearly, you do *not erase* your [old] thinking." Thinking is not wrong in the sense that it fails to correspond to the physical reality or the mental content given in a metaphysical sense or in experiential purity/certitude, since there is no such foundation behind or outside the thinking itself—this is indeed radical "perspectivism." More important for our subject matter at hand, however, is the notion that the so-called wrong thinking amounts to a temporary deviation, which is invariably *within* the reason of Dharma-nature, never outside.

Perhaps the most controversial presupposition of such religious hermeneutics as Dōgen's is that a wrong view or an evil act is, in essence, a *misguided striving for reason*. That is to say, for all its misguidedness, it is nevertheless a striving for reason, or is reason's striving, if you will. As such, the reason in Dharma-nature embraces, rather than abandons, this misguided striving; to do otherwise would amount to compromising its logic as well as its efficaciousness in Zen soteriology.[33] Thus, Dōgen recommends illumining and penetrating, rather than obliterating, the old, in order to create the new. Could this inclusivist viewpoint of understanding stand up to those strictures which most often point to tendencies in Zen to incapacitate and disregard the proper exercise of criticism?

For Dōgen's part, he has this to say earlier in the same "Hosshō" fascicle:

> The sūtras are Dharma-nature and hence one's self; competent teachers are Dharma-nature and hence one's self. Because Dharma-nature is one's self, it is not a kind of self that is erroneously conceived by non-Buddhists and fiendish thugs. There is no room for non-Buddhists and fiendish thugs! There is no room for non-Buddhists and fiendish thugs in Dharma-nature!

Let me provide readers with a textual background for this quotation: Dōgen maintains that even though humans may have a "natural capability/preparedness to discern" (*shōchi*) Dharma-nature, they must *cultivate* it by studying the sūtras and following competent teachers. Ultimately all that amounts to "enlightenment-by-oneself without a teacher" (*mushi dokugo*) and, as such, is nothing but Dharma-nature's activity itself. Dōgen's above-quoted strong disapproval is made in view of such an antecedent thesis. Now that we have here encountered Dōgen's exclusivist view, which seems to totally reject the faulty thinking of self, our question is: Is Dōgen self-contradictory? Is there any way we can resolve the dilemma of the inclusivist and exclusivist views that were presented in the same fascicle?

My reading of the text under consideration is this: Dōgen's critique, however "exclusivist," caustic and denunciatory in its tenor and rhetoric, is always grounded in, and tempered by, his "inclusivist" hermeneutics of understanding. Even so, the force and sharpness of his utterances are never marred by the guise of an uncritical, holistic hermeneutics. In this light, what matters in the reason of Dharma-nature is the practitioner's obligation to negotiate the Way at the interface of *understanding* and *criticism*—not inclusivism and exclusivism as such—and use them as the foci of practice. That is to say, embracing a misguided striving for reason should in no way constitute approving it, or acceding to it. Nevertheless, the reason of Dharma-nature, in the final analysis, remains bottomlessly elusive (*mutan*), as ever.[34]

7

I have sometimes referred to Dōgen as a thinker *and* a visionary. By this I do not imply any bifurcatory framework in which thinking and vision coexist amicably, and yet, are two different faculties of the mind. This view dichotomously distinguishes between one as cognitive/objective and the other as emotive/subjective. As noted so far, thinking and vision for Dōgen permeate each other and collaborate in and through the body-mind.

Consider Dōgen's statement about a painted picture (*gato*; *ga*):

> My late master [Ju-ching] once said: "A tall bamboo and a [short] banana plant are together embodied as a painted picture."
>
> This utterance is such that although it refers to that which transcends tallness and shortness, it attests to a deep meditation on both [the bamboo and the banana plant] *embodied as a painted picture.* . . .
>
> All the foregoing features of the tall bamboo and the banana plant are, in themselves, pictures. Accordingly, for a person who is greatly enlightened upon hearing the sound of [a pebble hitting] bamboo [as Hsiang-yen Chih-hsien experienced], an authority and a beginner [in spiritual matters] are equally pictures. You should not doubt it by erroneously construing ordinary people and the buddhas [as different from one another]. [As an ancient once said,] "How tall that bamboo is! How short this bamboo is! How tall this bamboo is! How short that bamboo is!" Because all are pictures, the tall ones and the short ones always fit with one another. If there are pictures of the tall, this does not mean that there are no pictures of the short. You should penetratingly investigate this truth. Because the entire universe and all things are, as such, pictures, both humans and things actualize themselves through pictures. The Buddha-ancestors perfect themselves through pictures.[35]

The *Shōbōgenzō*, "Gabyō" fascicle (1242), from which the foregoing quotation derives, is traditionally interpreted primarily from the standpoint of nonduality and equality. It has thus been understood that all beings and things as painted pictures are equal in spiritual status. Such egalitarianism aside, there is something more vitally important for our understanding of reason—the *multiplicity* of pictures. The word *picture* is not merely equalized in its generic sense, but polysemous in its infinite varieties. Thus, a tall bamboo and a short banana plant are each embodied as, or present in and through, a painted picture (*gato ni iru*); likewise, only as such, are they pictures. One picture or many pictures are all engendered by the activity of painting or picturing, by way of the painter's (the practitioner's) creative imagination.

Elsewhere, Dōgen makes his thesis more explicit in his analysis of Ju-ching's statement that in part says, "The spring is present in and through the plum blossoms and is embodied as a painted picture . . . ":

> The spring we are talking about now is the *painted* spring because it is "em-bodied as a painted picture." This has nothing to do with any extraneous powers but only *allows* the plum blossoms to *exert* the spring; this is why [the spring] is painted in the picture and enters the [plum] tree. They are all skillful means.[36]

As shown here, the spring and the plum blossoms—life and art, truth and the imagination, or the one and the many, if you will—are never bifurcated as some modern thinkers might uncritically assume, but constitute a total reality in which the spring is realized as a painted picture via the plum blossoms and the painter's striving. The painted picture "allows the plum blossoms to exert the spring" and thereby the spring "enters the [plum] tree." This whole dynamic is neither a revelation, nor an invention, nor a discovery; rather it is what Dōgen calls the "opening up and illumining" (*kaimei*) of a salvific reality as a painted picture. Thus reality is picture, picture is reality.

In a similar vein, Dōgen has this to say further:

> An ancient buddha once said: "Enlightenment is attained; white snow cov-ers the earth far and wide. Painting the blue mountains [buried under snow] is completed in a scroll."
>
> This is a talk of great enlightenment and indicates the realized state of practicing and studying the Way. Thus, right at the moment when you attain enlightenment, you *designate* the blue mountains and white snow as a picture scroll; *you have been painting* the picture of them. There is not a single activity, just as it is, that is not a picture. Our present endeavor is made pos-sible solely by virtue of a picture.[37]

Because you "designate" the blue mountains and white snow—and by ex-tension, all things of the universe—as "a picture scroll," and because "you have been painting the picture of them" throughout your life, you are the sole agent who paints or pictures (*gato su*) the universe, as well as the self.[38] A notable implication, analogous to that of the reason of Dharma-nature as seen before, is that from the shaman's mystical flight to the philosopher's abstruse system, from the devotee's relic veneration to the dharmologian's dharmic discourse, all beliefs and practices, myths and rituals—valid or in-valid—are invariably the products of our hermeneutic efforts to picture the self and the world. In pictures Dōgen sees the common thread, as well as the differences, of all human beings' diverse enterprises. More importantly, however, picturing the world *is* a legitimate mode of thinking.

Consider the creative process of painting:

> To paint a landscape, you use blue and green paints, rare boulders, extraordinary rocks, or the seven jewels and the four treasures; the same is true of the task of painting a cake. To paint a picture of a person, you choose the four elements and the five *skandhas*; to paint a picture of the Buddha, you choose not only a clay shrine and an earthen image but the thirty-two marks, a blade of grass, and countless kalpas of assiduous practice. Because you have been painting the Buddha in such a manner, all the buddhas are, without exception, the painted pictures of the buddhas; all the painted pictures of the buddhas are none other than all the [real] buddhas. Examine a painted picture of the Buddha and a painted picture of a cake. Which one is a stone-carved tortoise? Which one is an iron staff? [Which one is a representation? Which one is a thing? Both are real.] Which one is material, and which one is mental? You should carefully consider these questions and investigate them thoroughly. When you endeavor in this way, [you will realize that] life and death, their comings and goings, are all painted pictures/painting pictures; supreme enlightenment is indeed a painted picture/painting a picture. All the dharma world and the empty sky—there is nothing whatsoever that is not painting a picture/a painted picture.[39]

I wish to briefly note three points: (1) A picture is not a representation of reality in the philosophical sense; to understand this, the dualism of reality and representation must collapse. Even so, the process of painting a picture is not arbitrary, capricious, or undisciplined but informed and nurtured by cultural sensibilities and personal/historical memories, among a number of other conditions. The painting process is thinking. For Dōgen, of course, the conditions and reasons that are instrumental to bringing a picture into being are coextensive with one's self and the entire world. (2) Dōgen once wrote: "The monastics of future generations will be able to understand one-taste Zen based on words and letters, if they devote efforts to spiritual practice by seeing the universe through words and letters, and words and letters through the universe."[40] Replace "words and letters" in the above passage with "pictures," and its gist is the same—the reason is that for Dōgen, picture *is* language and language *is* picture. Both in turn belong to thinking. Thus the visual and linguistic, the spatial and temporal, imagination and conceptualization, the material and mental, the sensuous and rational coalesce in Dōgen's religious method and hermeneutics.

(3) Today, the sharp dichotomy between picture as spontaneous, immediate, emotive, and private, and language as restrictive, abstract, cognitive, and public, has largely been challenged as untenable.[41] For Dōgen's part, visual/spatial thinking and linguistic/temporal thinking are inseparably intertwined with one another in their shared endeavors to "understand the Way through the body-mind" (*shinjin gakudō*). Together they constitute the *kernel* of Zen realization—neither at the core nor on the surface.

8

In discussing the Buddhist saying, "One who falls because of the ground rises always because of the very ground," Dōgen approves of its general purport, but as usual, offers a biting cautionary note:

> Because of the [Buddhists'] failure to penetratingly study this saying through practice, they understand it only in terms of "like this," and not in terms of "not like this." Even though the ancient buddha's dictum has come down to us in this way, when you yourself as an ancient buddha listen to that ancient buddha's saying, your query should go beyond it. [Such a query as yours] may never have been addressed in India or in the world of gods; for all that, it is reasonable for you to speak it. Then, if one who falls because of the ground wants to be raised up by the very ground, one can never stand up even after countless kalpas. Rising can only happen through a singular liberating momentum. That is to say, "one who falls because of the ground rises always because of the sky, and one who falls because of the sky rises always because of the ground." If this were not the case, one's rising would never be possible. All the buddhas, all the ancestors have lived in this manner, without exception.[42]

I think this passage is quite fitting in closing this chapter. However self-evident the ancient saying in question may be, there is no excuse for practitioners not to challenge it, examine it, or negate it, because not to do so is insufficient. Negation in Mahāyāna Buddhism, as noted before, signifies neither the absence nor the removal of what is negated. "Like this" (*immo*) and "not like this" (*fu-immo*) are the foci, so to speak, that are engaged in the dynamic, dialectical relationship of informing, challenging, and renewing each other in their nonduality.

By the same token, "the ground" needs "not the ground" in order to become genuinely, soterically efficacious. From this perspective, Dōgen speaks of "a singular liberating momentum" (*hitotsu no katsuro*) by way of referring to the sky, as "not the ground." The ground and the sky, though separated as far away as "108,000 *ri*" as Dōgen puts it, are indispensable to one another in their shared soteriological enterprise and by virtue of the potency of emptiness. Their intimacy is such that "If you fall because of the ground, you rise always because of the sky, and it is altogether impossible to rise apart from the sky; if you fall because of the sky, you rise always because of the ground, and it is altogether impossible to rise apart from the ground."[43]

In the context of the present chapter, this recast dictum is enormously important. The singular liberating momentum as the transformative power of emptiness goes beyond the ground and the sky only in and through the immersion of itself in their concurrence and reciprocation. Conversely, it penetrates that relationship only by going beyond them. In such an interplay, the sky and the ground are farther than the farthest and nearer than the nearest. This is the elusive subtlety of their intimacy. Analogously, in the world where nothing is intrinsically rational or irrational, the same holds true of the deconstructive and reconstructive functions of emptiness with respect to reason. The full authentication and empowerment of reason require both functions in praxis. This is what I would call "radical reason" in Dōgen's Zen.

Postscript

In these six short chapters, I have presented some salient facets of Dōgen's thought on authentic practice, which was his paramount concern in his praxis-oriented Zen. In this regard, his emphasis was on the reconstructive use of such notions as duality in relation to nonduality and dependent origination in relation to emptiness. His thrust was as much on engagement in duality as it was on nonattachment to duality. Thus Dōgen located his religious method and hermeneutics in the clear understanding and responsible use of language, thinking, and reason. The present work's primary purpose has been to explicate such a methodological/hermeneutic orientation and its significance. This orientation, as I see it, was the common thread running through Dōgen's *Shōbōgenzō* (as well as his other writings), although it evolved throughout his monastic career before reaching its final form later in life—most notably in relation to his notion of nonthinking.

Authentic practice in its simplest terms consists of dialectically negotiating the Way—between nonduality and duality, between the unitive vision of all things and the revalorized world of daily life, between enlightenment and practice, and between ultimate truth and worldly truth. All of these pairs are the foci in the process of one's realization. The authenticity in question does not lie in assent to any beliefs or conformity to any rules and principles, but rather in living dynamically and dialogically through the interplay of those salvific foci in any given situation.

Through such a highly unorthodox formulation of Zen method and hermeneutics, Dōgen (1) offers a new direction in Zen praxis with a number of important implications, and (2) opens up new possibilities for creative dialogue between Zen and contemporary thought. By way of concluding this present work, I would like to make a few final observations on these two points.

1. Dōgen's instructions on seated meditation were brief and minimalist. He did not elaborate on meditation techniques or meditative experiences in any detail, nor did he attempt to guide his disciples through graduated stages of meditative and spiritual progression, as we often see in some religious traditions within and without Buddhism. I do not attribute his peculiar instructional style to any insensitivity toward his disciples' soteric welfare. Rather, his approach emerged from his foremost desire to provide them with fundamental principles—spelled out in terms of language, thinking, and reason—with which each could grapple with his/her individual soteric project, thereby realizing his/her *own* Zen. Dōgen demonstrated this himself by writing the fascicles of the *Shōbōgenzō*.

To illustrate, consider "enlightenment-by-oneself without a teacher" (*mushi dokugo*), the ultimate Zen principle that every practitioner had to actualize, even while studying under competent teachers and reading the sūtras for a number of years.[1] Dōgen provided this well-known dictum with a specific methodological/hermeneutic key that allowed one to unlock the mystery of existence—that is, to open the self and the universe. That key amounted, in essence, to critical, reflective thinking as an integral part of meditation. Without this key, it was impossible to attain one's own salvific independence.

Thus, however much a meditative experience might strike one as indubitably immediate and certain, that experience alone does not warrant a person the authenticity of practice. Through his notion of nonthinking, Dōgen was equally critical of the same self-aggrandizing potentiality of wisdom. Meditation and wisdom alike had to be subjected to critical scrutiny and reassessed in the changing situation. Accordingly, he underscored that Zen which is reexpressed and reconceived by each individual practitioner and by each generation, according to different conditions and needs. Zen's so-called fierce individualism is, in this way, firmly grounded in one's existential situation: Each practitioner must add his/her own details. Nevertheless, within the purview of his egalitarianism, Dōgen's demand was uncompromisingly elitist.

This methodological characteristic was also a direct challenge to Zen's famously transgressive, antiauthoritarian, and iconoclastic temperament. This is not to say that it was no longer usable or relevant, but rather that it had to be informed and tempered by concerns with the temporality of existence-time (*uji*). For Dōgen, the matter had less to do with liberation from intellectual constraints, and more to do with the engagement in the existential predicament. His stance, therefore, was far from a disclaimer of reveling in playfulness of image making or in religious, mythopoeic imagination.

Quite the contrary. For instance, when Dōgen discussed Dharma-nature's reason (*hosshō no dōri*), he juxtaposed it with Dharma-nature's *samādhi* (*hosshō zammai*). Reason and *samādhi* went together in Dharma-nature.[2] Traditional Zen's iconoclasm was thus empowered, rather than disowned, by Dōgen's insistence on the bold, yet humble, use of images (icons) as a necessary tool of authentic thinking. Herein we find Dōgen's egalitarianism unscathed despite his elitist demand, as noted above.

2. For all the enormous contrasts between Dōgen's world and our world (filled with incredible scientific achievements, virtual reality, insatiable consumerism, and so forth), many of us are still struck by his remarkably modern sensibility to language and critical thinking. Yet we must nevertheless realize that his entire religio-philosophical thought operates by way of his thoroughly praxis-oriented Zen soteriology and eclectic Mahāyāna worldview, as well as through the ethos of medieval Japan in the thirteenth century. For this reason, promises and perils always lurk in any genuine attempt to engage in dialogue with Dōgen.

He, more often than not, challenges us on many fronts to think through a great number of assumptions, for example, with respect to language and reality, matter and spirit, and self and world. To cite just one example, he issued a strong warning against the anthropocentric conception of human language. For Dōgen, human language was neither more nor less than one of the infinite varieties of language (*monji*) and expression (*dōtoku*) in the universe. Despite his insistence on the imperativeness of human language in his soteric project, Dōgen never lost sight of the larger picture in which human and nonhuman beings engaged in an ongoing communion through their respective languages/expressions. Farfetched as it may seem, this was his vision of the universe in which all beings—living *and* nonliving—engage in a shared salvific project, through their "vast, giddy karmic consciousnesses." In this view, Dōgen's linguistic stance cannot and should not be facilely equated to, or explained away by, certain modern philosophical views and notions.

Incidentally, although the notion of "the grand narrative," or "the grand picture" if you will, as in the foregoing vision, is in disrepute in our postmodern age, it was quite legitimate, and even necessary, in Dōgen's linguistic universe. For this reason, the whole picture of Buddha-nature, for instance, remained pivotal in his soteriology despite all the problems alleged by its critics. Remember that in his Zen, Buddha-nature, for all its seeming grandeur, is thoroughly impermanent. Yet precisely for this reason, it is able to orient and catalyze authentic practice in a manner most appropriate to its soteric workings.

Now, let me briefly touch upon the ethical aspect of Dōgen's religion. Contrary to the view of some critics who hold that Dōgen had little or no social ethic, I would argue, as I did in my writings, that his monastic way of life was as socially engaged as, say, Nichiren's or Shinran's religions in Kamakura Japan. It is high time for us to appreciate the *social* significance of Dōgen's monasticism. At the very least, even silence and quietude in the monastic life can be regarded as the forms of social activism.

Having said that, I would further contend that we do not find social ethics of a *modern* variety in Dōgen—that is, the systemic and ideological critique of institutions and policies with respect to the state and society at large, and even the global community, in terms of such socioeconomic and political problems as poverty, race, class, family, violence, and human rights. This is the typical modern sensibility—broadly called social justice—that arose largely along with the Industrial Revolution, although closely allied ideologically with the Enlightenment which itself has now been severely challenged by postmodern critique. Our modern sensibility, still in constant evolution, was simply nonexistent in Dōgen's age and culture. Such a "disadvantage" was the case not only with Japan but with all *premodern* traditions, including religions. For better or worse, such an awareness has had a tremendous impact on all the traditional religions throughout the world. Thus in this particular respect, Dōgen was a product of medieval Japan. To a great extent, his limitation *was* Japanese culture's limitation at the time.

However, this observation should by no means minimize the enormous potential of Dōgen's seminal methodological/hermeneutic ideas for personal and social ethics today. In fact, I would suggest, by following Friedrich Schleiermacher's wise counsel, that it is our obligation—whether we are Zen practitioners or not—to understand Dōgen's insights better than he did himself. From this perspective, his religio-philosophical groundwork not only offers a new direction in Zen praxis but also opens up new possibilities for creative dialogue between Zen and contemporary thought, especially regarding social ethics, to which modern Zen by and large has been sadly impervious.

We live in a profoundly crisis-ridden age in human history. In an apocalyptic world, we all seem helplessly caught between despair and hope. What is hope? What can we hope for? Is there any hope for hope at all? These are the questions we struggle with today. For Dōgen's part, he quietly calls for authentic practice.

Glossary of Sino-Japanese Words, Names, and Titles

Abe Masao　阿部正雄
aigo　愛語
akiramu　あきらむ / 明らむ / 諦む
Akiyama Hanji　秋山範二
aku shiyui　惡思惟
Amida　阿彌陀
ango / "Ango"　安居
arakan / "Arakan"　阿羅漢
baika / "Baika"　梅華
bendō　辨(辨)道
Bendōhō　辨(辨)道法
"Bendōwa"　辨(辨)道話
bōko　慕古
bokuseki shin　木石心
bukka　佛果
bukkyō / "Bukkyō" (34)　佛敎
bukkyō / "Bukkyō" (47)　佛經
buppō no dōri　佛法の道理
busshō / "Busshō"　佛性
busso kōmyō　佛祖光明
busso no riero　佛祖の 理會路
butsu　佛
Butsudō akiramezareba busshi ni arazu. Busshi to iuwa busshi to iu kotonari
　佛道あきらめざれば, 佛嗣にあらず. 佛嗣といふは, 佛子といふこ
　となり
butsuin　佛因
butsuryō　佛量
byōdō　不等
byōdō soku shabetsu　不等卽差別
Ch'an　禪
Ch'ang-lu Tsung-tse　長盧宗賾
Ch'ang-sha Ching-ts'en　長沙景岑

Chao-chio Ch'ang-tsung　照覺常總
Chi ni yorite taoruru mono wa kanarazu chi ni yorite oku
　　　地によりて たふるるものは，かならず 地によりておく
Chiang-si Ma-tsu　江西馬祖
chie no Bukkyō　智慧の佛教
chikaku　知覺
chinchō izen no kōan　朕兆已前之公案
Ching-chao　京兆
chōnyū　跳入
chōshutsu　跳出
Chu　竺
Ch'uan-fa yüan　傳法院
Chuang-tzu　莊子
chūdō　中道
dadei taisui　拕泥 滯水
daigo / "Daigo"　大悟
daimei　大迷
Dainichibō Nōnin　大日房能忍
daishugyō / "Daishugyō"　大修行
darani / "Darani"　陀羅尼
datsuraku　脱落
dō (tao)　道
Dōgen　道元
Dōgen Zen　道元禪
dōri　道理
dōshin　道心
dōtoku / "Dōtoku"　道得
e　慧
Echizen　越前
ei　翳
eigen　翳眼
engi　緣起
en'in kaman　圓因果滿
fudōtoku　不道得
fuhitsu　不必
fuichi fui　不一不異
fu-immo　不恁麼
Fukan zazengi　普勸坐禪儀
Fukui　福井
fumai inga　不昧因果
fumbetsu　分別
fumbetsu-chi　分別智
funi　不二

funi fuichi   不二不一
fu-shiryō   不思量
fuzenna   不染汚
fuzenna no shushō   不染汚の修證
ga   畫
gabyō / "Gabyō"   畫餅
gato   畫圖
Ge wa ge o sae ge o miru. Ge wa ge o gesuru nari, kore toki nari
    礙は礙をさへ礙をみる.礙は礙を礙するなり, これ時なり
gen   眼
gen'ei   眼翳
gengen hempon   還源返本
genjō   現成
genjō kōan / "Genjō kōan"   現成公案(按)
go   悟
gō   業
gongo dōdan   言語道斷
goppō no dōri   業報の道理
goryō   悟量
gosshiki bōbō / bōbō gosshiki   業識茫茫 / 茫茫業識
gūjin   究盡
gūjin no dōri   究盡の道理
gyō / katachi   形
gyōbutsu iigi / "Gyōbutsu iigi"   行佛威儀
gyōji / "Gyōji"   行持
gyōnyo   形如
Hakamaya Noriaki   袴谷憲昭
hakarai   はからひ
hakaru   量る
hakyō   破鏡
hasshōdō   八聖(正)道
hei   平
henkai fuzōzō   遍(徧)界不曾藏
Hiei   比叡
higan tō   彼岸到
hihan Bukkyō   批判佛教
hiniku kotsuzui   皮肉骨髓
hiniku kotsuzui no kattō suru dōri   皮肉骨髓の葛藤する道理
Hisamatsu Shin'ichi   久松眞一
hi-shiryō   非思量
hitotsu no katsuro   ひとつの活路
hitsuzen naru   必然なる
hō (fa)   法

hōbemmon　方便門
hōben　方便
hōben hossin　方便法身
hōben sesshō　方便殺生
hōi　法位
hōjutsu　法術
hokkai　法界
hokkairyō　法界量
Hokke　法華
hōnen　法然
hongaku　本覺
hongaku shisō　本覺思想
hōni dōri　法爾道理
honshō myōshu　本證妙修
hōryō　法量
hosshō / "Hōsshō"　法性
hosshō no baku　法性の縛
hōtō　寶塔
Hsiang-yen Chih-hsien　香巖智閑
Hsiu-ching　休靜
Huang-po　黃檗
Hua-yen　華嚴
Hui-k'o　慧可
Hung-chih Cheng-chüeh　宏智正覺
ichimizen　一味禪
ichimoku rai no gotoshi　一默如雷
ichinyo　一如
ichizu　一圖
immo / "Immo"　恁麼
inga no dōri　因果の道理
ippō gūjin　一法究盡
Ippō o shōsuru toki wa ippō wa kurashi
　　一方を證するときは, 一方はくらし
isō　已曾
isō fumbetsu　已曾分別
issai shujō shitsuu busshō / issai no shujō wa kotogotoku busshō ari
　　一切衆生悉有佛性
issaihō isshin　一切法一心
issendai　一闡提
Izutsu Toshihiko　井筒俊彦
ja shiryō　邪思量
ja shiyui　邪思惟
jiji muge (shih-shih wu-ai)　事事無礙

jijuyū zammai　自受用三昧
jiko kōmyō　自己光明
jiko no toki naru dōri　自己の時なる道理
jin jippōkai　盡十方界
jindaichi no kokoro　盡大地の心
jinen　自然
jinen gedō　自然外道
jinen hōni　自然法爾
jinen ni　自然に
jinshin inga / "Jinshin inga"　深信因果
jinsoku　神足
jinzū / "Jinzū"　神通
jippō shiyui　十方思惟
jiri　自利
jisetsu innen　時節因緣
jishō　自性
jō　定
jōgu bodai geke shujō　上求菩提下化衆生
jōroku konjin　丈六金身
jōryō　情量
Ju-ching　如淨
juki / "Juki"　授記
ka / nani　何
ka kokū / kokū ni kakaru　掛虛空
kahitsu　何必
kaiin zammai / "Kaiin zammai"　海印三昧
kai-jō-e　戒定慧
kaimei　開明
kaitō tennō　廻頭轉腦
kaku　覺
kakusha　覺者
Kamakura　鎌倉
kanna zen　看話禪
Karoku　嘉祿
katsuro　活路
kattō / "Kattō"　葛藤
Kedashi musō-zammai no katachi mangetsu no gotoku naru o motte nari
　　蓋以無相三昧形如滿月
Kegon (Hua-yen)　華嚴
Kegon kyō　華嚴經
keige　罣礙
keisei sanshoku / "Keisei sanshoku"　谿(溪)聲山色
kembutsu / "Kembutsu"　見佛

kesetsu   假設(說)

kishi   旣至

kōdō zen   皇道禪

kōjō   向上

kokū / "Kokū"   虛空

kokū no keijū   虛空の輕重

kokū no naige   虛空の內外

kokū no sakkatsu   虛空の殺活

kokyō / "Kokyō"   古鏡

Komazawa   駒澤

kōmyō / "Kōmyō"   光明

konchin   昏沈

konjin   渾人

kono hō no okoru toki / shihō kiji   此法起時

konshin   渾身 / 渾心

konshinjin   渾身心

Kōroku / Eihei kōroku   廣錄 / 永平廣錄

kosoku kōan   古則公案

kotowari   ことわり/ことはり/ 理 / 處

kū   空

kū ni kakareri   空にかかれり

kū ze kū   空是空

kūge / "Kūge"   空華

kūgō izen no shushō   空劫已前之修證

kyakumei   却迷

kyōkan   經卷

kyōryaku   經歷

kyōsō hanjaku / kyōhan   教相判釋 / 教判

Lao-tzu   老子

Lin-chi   臨濟

Lu-shan   廬山

maka hannya haramitsu / "Maka hannya haramitsu"   摩訶般若波羅蜜

makumōzō   莫妄想

mappō   末法

Matsumoto Shirō   松本史朗

meigo   迷悟

meigo ichinyo   迷悟一如

mitsu   密

mitsugo / "Mitsugo"   密語

mochiiru   もちゐる

mō-fumbetsu   妄分別

mokushō zen   默照禪

monji   文字

monji no dōri   文字の道理

monjo no dōtoku   問處の道得

Moshi shosō wa hisō nari to mireba sunawachi nyorai o miru nari / moshi shosō
　　　to hisō too mireba . . .   若見諸相非相卽見如來

mu / yume   夢

mu-busshō   無佛性

muchū setsumu / "Muchū setsumu"   夢中說夢

mu-fumbetsu-chi   無分別智

mugen hōyō   夢幻泡影

muhon kakyo   無本可據

mujō seppō / "Mujō seppō"   無情說法

mujō-busshō   無常佛性

munen (wu-nien)   無念

musa muchū   夢作夢中

mushi dokugo   無師獨悟

mushin (wu-hsin)   無心

mutan   無端

myōin   妙因

myōka   妙果

Nakamura Hajime   中村元

Nan-ch'üan   南泉

Nan-yang Hui-chung   南陽慧忠

Nan-yüeh Huai-jang   南嶽懷讓

nenkaku   念覺

nenryo   念慮

nichigetsu seishin shin   日月星辰心

Nichiren   日蓮

Nihon Daruma shū   日本達磨宗

nihonjinron   日本人論

nihonshugi   日本主義

nikon   而今

nikon tōsho / ima itaru tokoro ni   而今到處

ninnin no dōri   任任の道理

ninryō   人量

Nishida Kitarō   西田幾太郎

Nishitani Keiji   西谷啓治

nyakushi   若至

nyo / gotoku   如

nyoraizō   如來藏

nyoze   如是

onorezukara   おのれづから

onozukara   おのづから/自ら

ōsaku sendaba / "Ōsaku sendaba"   王索仙陀婆

P'an-shan Pao-chi   盤山寶積
Pao-chih   寶智
Pi-yen lu   碧巖錄
rakka   落花
Rekinen to shite watakushi nashi   歷然として わたくしなし
ri   里
ri (li)   理
ri-busshō   理佛性
ri-hosshin   理法身
riji muge (li-shih wu-ai)   理事無礙
rinyū   理入
rita   利他
rodōdō   露堂堂
rokudō   六道
ryō   量
ryochi   慮知
ryochi nenkaku   慮知念覺
ryōshō tasshi   了生達死
ryōsu   量す
ryūgin / "Ryūgin"   龍吟
sabutsu   作佛
san ze san   山是山
sanjigō / "Sanjigō"   三時業
sanjūshichihon bodaibumpō / "Sanjūshichihon bodaibumpō"
        三十七品菩提分法
sansuikyō / "Sansuikyō"   山水經
satori   さとり/悟 / 覺 / 證
senga daichi shin   山河大地心
senni gedō   先尼外道
setsuna shōmetsu no dōri   剎那生滅の道理
shabetsu   差別
shi shimo-butsu immorai   是什麼物恁麼來
shichibutsu tsūkaige   七佛通戒偈
shigetsu   指月
Shih-t'ou Hsi-ch'ien   石頭希遷
shikan taza   只(祇)管打坐
shikiryōsu   測量す
shimmitsu   親密
shimo   祇麼 / 只麼
shin   心
shinfukatoku   心不可得
shingyō shometsu   心行處滅
shinjin   身心

shinjin datsuraku   身心脱落
shinjin datsuraku   心塵脱落
shinjin gakudō / "Shinjin gakudō"   身心學道
shinjō sōmetsu   心常相滅
shinnyo   眞如
shinnyo hosshin   眞如法身
Shinran   親鸞
shinzō   親曾
shiryō   思量
shisho / "Shisho"   嗣書
shitsuu   悉有
shiyōsuru   使用する
shiyui   思惟
shiyui jinsoku   思惟神足
shizen biku / "Shizen biku"   四禪比丘
shō   證
shoaku makusa / "Shoaku makusa"   諸惡莫作
Shōbōgenzō   正法眼藏
Shobutsu kore shō naru yueni shobutsu kore shō nari
        諸佛これ證なるゆゑに, 諸物これ證なり
shōchi   生知
shō-fumbetsu   正分別
shohō jissō / "Shohō jissō"   諸法實相
shōji / "Shōji"   生死
shōshi   正思
shō-shiryō   正思量
shō-shiyui   正思惟
shōtō immoji   正當恁麼時
shō-zō-matsu no sanji   正像末の三時
shunjū / "Shunjū"   春秋
shushō   修證
shushō ittō / shushō ichinyo   修證一等 / 修證一如
shutsuro   出路
soku   卽
sokuhi no ronri   卽非の論理
sokuryo gyōjaku   息慮凝寂
sokushin jōbutsu   卽身成佛
sokushin zebutsu / "Sokushin zebutsu"   卽心是佛
somo   作麼
sōmu fumbetsu   曾無分別
Sōtō Zen   曹洞禪
Su Tung-p'o   蘇東坡
sui ze sui   水是水

Sung　宋
Suzuki Daisetz T.　鈴木大拙
Ta-chien Hui-neng　大鑑慧能
Ta-erh　大耳
taiki seppō　對機說法
Takasaki Jikidō　高崎直道
T'ang　唐
Tao-fu　道副
Tao-yü　道育
tare　誰 / たれ
tariki　他力
tashintsū / "Tashintsū"　他心通
Tempuku　天福
Tendai (T'ien-t'ai)　天台
tennen gedō　天然外道
Tenzo kyōkun　典座敎訓
Terada Tōru　寺田透
tōdatsu　透脱
tō-higan　到彼岸
tōkan jisetsu innen　當觀時節因緣
tōtai datsuraku　透體脱落
Tōtoku anokutara sammyaku sambodai / masani anokutara sammyaku sambodai
　　o ubeshi　當得阿耨多羅 三藐三菩提
Ts'an-t'ung-ch'i　參同契
Tso-ch'an chen　坐禪箴
Tso-ch'an i　坐禪儀
tsuki / "Tsuki"　都機
Tsung-chih　總持
Tung-shan　洞山
tzu-jan　自然
u-busshō　有佛性
udonge / "Udonge"　優曇華
uji / "Uji" / arutoki　有時
Yo no naka wa nani ni tatoen mizutori no hashifuru tsuyu ni yadoru tsukikage
　　世中は何にたとへん 水鳥の, はしふる露にやどる月影
yōjutsu　要術
Yü　禹
Yüan-wu K'o-ch'in　圜悟克勤
Yüeh-shan Wei-yen　藥山惟儼
yuishiki shisō　唯識思想
yuke　遊化
Yün-men Wen-yen　雲門文偃
zazen　坐禪

zazen no Bukkyō   坐禪の佛敎
zazenshin / "Zazenshin"   坐禪箴
ze   是
zen / Zen (Ch'an)   禪
zengyō hōben   善巧方便
zenki / "Zenki"   全機
zeshin sabutsu   是心作佛
zōji tempai   造次顛沛
zu   圖
zu-sabutsu   圖作佛

Notes

Preface

1. Hee-Jin Kim, *Dōgen Kigen—Mystical Realist*, Monograph 29 of the Association for Asian Studies (Tucson: University of Arizona Press, 1975); *Dōgen Kigen: Mystical Realist* (revised edition, 1987); *Eihei Dōgen: Mystical Realist*, the Wisdom edition (Boston: Wisdom Publications, 2004).

2. Of the six, chapters 1–3, 5, and 6 are newly written for this present work. Chapter 4 is adapted from a previously published article, with some minor changes and deletions.

3. Herbert Fingarette, *Confucius—The Secular as Sacred*, pp. 57–70.

4. Confucius, *The Analects of Confucius* (trans. Arthur Waley), II.1.

Chapter 1. A Shattered Mirror, a Fallen Flower

1. For my exposition of Dōgen's Zen in the present work, I have decided to use "foci" in place of conventional terms such as "opposites," "antitheses," and "polarities," in order to underscore the fact that the word "focus/foci" is employed *soteriologically*, not as a metaphysical, explanatory, theoretical, or descriptive designation. Opposites and antitheses are often associated with teleological, essentialist, epistemological, and ontological interests and frameworks; tend to be static and abstract; and are concerned with substratum, entity, ground, source, etc. By contrast, foci refer to those designations, usually in pairs, that are employed to do something—in our case, to do religion, to attain liberation. The usefulness of this hermeneutic notion in the context of Dōgen's Zen will hopefully become clearer as we proceed in our discussion.

2. Dōgen, *Shōbōgenzō*, "Daigo." The *Shōbōgenzō* will be cited hereafter as S. For the original texts of Dōgen's *Shōbōgenzō*, I have used *Dōgen zenji zenshū*, vol. 1, ed. Ōkubo Dōshū, and *Dōgen*, 2 vols., ed. Terada Tōru and Mizuno Yaoko; for those of his other works, *Dōgen zenji zenshū*, vol. 2, ed. Ōkubo Dōshū.

3. *S*, "Daigo."

4. *Shinzō* is closely related to Dōgen's other notion *mitsugo* ("intimate words"). The idea of intimacy is crucially important here. More on this will follow in the subsequent chapters.

5. *S*, "Genjō kōan."

6. *S*, "Daigo."

7. *S*, "Muchū setsumu."

8. *S*, "Daigo."

9. Kim, *Eihei Dōgen: Mystical Realist*, pp. 16–18 concerning Dōgen's view on this doctrine. To Dōgen, every age was intrinsically crisis ridden, regardless of the so-called *mappō* thought.

10. This view is consonant with early Buddhist thought that the cause of both the arising and cessation of suffering is within suffering itself, and never outside. Walpola Rahula, *What the Buddha Taught*, pp. 31 and 42. See also chapter 6, section 8 of the present work regarding Dōgen's critique of this Buddhist dictum.

In this connection: "When a demon becomes a buddha, it exerts its demonness, breaks it, and actualizes a buddha. When a buddha becomes a buddha, he/she exerts his/her buddhahood, strives for it, and actualizes a buddha. When a human being becomes a buddha, he/she exerts his/her human nature, trains it, and actualizes a buddha. You should thoroughly understand the truth that possibilities [for actualizing a buddha] lie precisely in the ways [various beings] exert their respective natures." *S*, "Sanjūshichihon bodaibumpō."

11. *S*, "Daigo."

12. For the recasting of Socrates' aphorism, see H. Neill McFarland, *The Rush Hour of the Gods*, pp. 21–22.

13. Steven Heine, *The Zen Poetry of Dōgen: Verses from the Mountain of Eternal Peace*, p. 69.

14. For a general significance of Dōgen's view of impermanence, see Kim, op. cit., pp. 141–42.

15. *S*, "Kōmyō."

16. *S*, "Kōmyō." For Yün-men's kōan, see Urs App, *Master Yunmen: From the Record of the Chan Master "Gate of the Clouds*," nos. 143 and 245.

17. Thomas Cleary and J.C. Cleary, trans., *The Blue Cliff Record*, vol. 3, p. 554.

18. Ibid., p. 555. Dōgen discusses P'an-shan's statement in his *S*, "Tsuki."

19. S, "Zazenshin."

20. Hee-Jin Kim, *Flowers of Emptiness: Selections from Dōgen's Shōbōgenzō*, p. 191, note 12.

21. S, "Muchū setsumu."

22. Kim, *Eihei Dōgen*, pp. 76–100. See also chapter 4 of the present work.

23. S, "Kūge."

24. Blaise Pascal, *Pascal's Pensées*, no. 414.

25. S, "Kūge."

26. S, "Kūge."

27. S, "Kūge."

28. Regarding this point, see Ōta Kyūki, "Hossō kyōgaku to Dōgen," in Kagamishima Genryū and Tamaki Kōshirō, eds., *Bukkyō kyōgaku to Dōgen* (*Kōza Dōgen*, no. 6), pp. 77–102. For consciousness-only thought, see Gadjin M. Nagao, *Mādhyamika and Yogācāra: A Study of Mahāyāna Philosophies*.

Chapter 2. Negotiating the Way

1. I am indebted to Norman Waddell and Masao Abe for the translation of *bendō* as "negotiating the Way." See Wadel and Abe, trans., *The Heart of Dōgen's Shōbōgenzō*, pp. 7–8.

2. Dōgen's question was: "As I study both the exoteric and the esoteric schools of Buddhism, they maintain that human beings are endowed with Dharma-nature by birth. If this is the case, why did the Buddhas of all ages—undoubtedly in possession of enlightenment—find it necessary to seek enlightenment and engage in spiritual practice?" The authenticity of this "great doubt" has been much debated by historians in Dōgen studies. See Kim, *Eihei Dōgen*, p. 22.

3. S, "Bendōwa."

4. S, "Bendōwa."

5. As for Dōgen's view on the analogy of ascent and descent in relation to the bodhisattva-way, see Kim, *Eihei Dōgen*, especially pp. 204–207.

6. See, for example, Ishii Shūdō, "Recent Trends in Dōgen Studies," in *Komazawa daigaku zen kenkyūjo nempō*, no. 1 (March 1990), pp. 219–64.

7. S, "Bendōwa."

8. S, "Gyōbutsu iigi."

9. C. W. Huntington, Jr., *The Emptiness of Emptiness: An Introduction to Early Indian Mādhyamika*, pp. 38ff., 47ff., 95ff., 108–109; p. 216, note 9; pp.232–33, note 47, on the two truths.

10. S, "Kokyō."

11. For recent discussion of the issues involved in the sudden-gradual model, see: Peter G. Gregory, ed., *Sudden and Gradual: Approaches to Enlightenment in Chinese Thought*. See also Bernard Faure, *The Rhetoric of Immediacy: A Cultural Critique of Chan/Zen Buddhism*.

12. S, "Zazenshin."

13. Dōgen was fond of using such expressions as *konshin* ("the whole body"), *konshin* ("the whole mind"), *konshinjin* ("the whole body-mind"), *konjin* ("the whole person"), and so forth. As clear from these expressions, Dōgen always spoke of the dynamic totality of the body-mind's cognitive, affective, and conative activities, and beyond.

14. S, "Zazenshin."

15. S, "Kattō."

16. S, "Kattō."

17. S, "Kembutsu," "Gyōbutsu iigi," "Shinjin gakudō," etc.

18. For a full-length treatment of the notion of skillful means, see Michael Pye, *Skillful Means: A Concept in Mahāyāna Buddhism*.

19. For example, see S, "Bodaisatta shishōhō."

20. This possibility suggests that the doctrine of skillful means should be carefully understood, especially in the context of controversies between the nihilist and absolutist readings of Mādhyamika thought. See Thomas E. Wood, *Nāgārjunian Disputations: A Philosophical Journey through an Indian Looking Glass*. In this book Wood defends the nihilist interpretation against the non-nihilist one.

21. S, "Ango."

22. S, "Shohō jissō." See also S, "Hokke ten Hokke."

23. Robert A. F. Thurman, trans., *The Holy Teaching of Vimalakīrti: A Mahāyāna Scripture*, chapter 9: "The Dharma-Door of Nonduality," pp. 73–77.

24. Ibid., p. 77.

25. S, "Sanjūshichihon bodaibumpō."

26. On the issue of experience in religious studies, see Robert H. Sharf, "Experience," in Mark C. Taylor, ed., *Critical Terms for Religious Studies*, pp. 94–116.

27. Robert H. Sharf, "Whose Zen? Zen Nationalism Revisited," in James W. Heisig and John C. Maraldo, eds., *Rude Awakenings: Zen, the Kyoto School, and the Question of Nationalism*, pp. 40–51; idem, "The Zen of Japanese Nationalism," in Donald S. Lopez, Jr., ed., *Curators of the Buddha: The Study of Buddhism under Colonialism*, pp. 107–60.

28. Bernard Faure, *Chan Insights and Oversights: An Epistemological Critique of the Chan Tradition*, chapter 2; idem, "The Kyoto School and Reverse Orientalism," in Charles Wei-hsun Fu and Steven Heine, eds., *Japan in Traditional and Postmodern Perspectives*, pp. 245–81.

29. John C. Maraldo, "Questioning Nationalism Now and Then: A Critical Approach to Zen and the Kyoto School," in Heisig and Maraldo, op. cit., pp. 333–62.

30. Fu and Heine, op. cit.

31. On Imperial Way Zen (*kōdō zen*), see Christopher Ives, "Ethical Pitfalls in Imperial Zen and Nishida Philosophy: Ichikawa Hakugen's Critique," in Heisig and Maraldo, op. cit., pp. 16–39.

32. Regarding the significance of "ever already" (*isō*), see chapter 5, section 3 below.

Chapter 3. Weighing Emptiness

1. D. T. Suzuki, *Zen and Japanese Culture*, p. 63.

2. Hee-Jin Kim, "'The Reason of Words and Letters': Dōgen and Kōan Language," in William R. LaFleur, ed., *Dōgen Studies*, pp. 54–82. See also chapter 4 of the present work.

3. *S*, "Muchū setsumu."

4. *S*, "Muchū setsumu."

5. *S*, "Muchū setsumu."

6. This logic in Dōgen's Zen is already familiar to us as we have seen in the saying: "One who falls because of the ground rises always because of the very ground." His metaphors of dim-sightedness (*eigen*), entwined vines (*kattō*), the flowers of emptiness (*kūge*), etc., show that thinking in one way or another: A deep immersion in elusive depths of duality and nonduality.

7. *S*, "Muchū setsumu."

8. *S*, "Kokū."

9. Hisamatsu Shin'ichi, "The Characteristics of Oriental Nothingness," *Philosophical Studies of Japan* 2 (1960), pp. 80–85.

10. *S*, "Zazenshin."

11. *S*, "Uji."

12. D. C. Lau, trans., *Lao Tzu: Tao Te Ching.*

13. *S*, "Zazenshin."

14. *S*, "Kokū."

15. *S*, "Maka hannya haramitsu."

16. Huntington calls "the emptiness of emptiness" "a self-deconstructing concept" in his op. cit., p. 132. Can emptiness stay in the transcendent state of ultimate truth and still be genuinely soteriological? This question will be addressed later in this chapter.

17. Cf. Terada Tōru, *Dōgen no gengo uchū*, p. 146.

18. Stephen Toulmin, *Human Understanding: The Collective Use and Evolution of Concepts*, p. x and p. 133. Toulmin in this work is concerned with the multiplicity of rational procedures, strategies, and standards accepted as authoritative in different cross-cultural, cross-epochal, and cross-disciplinary milieus. But what he says about rationality is quite relevant to our subject matter, although he is very much elitist in his approach.

19. This subject itself is enormously challenging in the contemporary situation. Right livelihood, one of the categories of the eightfold path, for example, does not remain to be merely a promotion of good and upright conduct on the part of an individual in making his or her livelihood, but should be concerned with the critique of, and efforts to address, the issues of capitalism which characterize the structure and dynamics of our nation and most of the other nations in the world today. Without this critical reflection, the notion of right livelihood is not only incomplete but ineffectual, for our lives are inextricably entangled with the realities of the global capitalist system with its exploitation, injustice, and ecological devastation. Thus capitalism has not just politico-economic but moral, religious implications. This is just an example of the weighing task that poses an enormous challenge in the modern situation.

20. Huntington, op. cit. This book is his exposition of Candrakīrti's *The Entry into the Middle Way (Madhyamakāvatāra).*

21. Ibid., pp. 39–40, 95–96.

22. Ibid., pp. 108–109.

23. For example, see ibid., pp. 69–104 on the ten perfections of the bodhisattva path.

24. The basic works of Critical Buddhism are: Matsumoto Shirō, *Engi to kū: nyoraizō shisō hihan*; Hakamaya Noriaki, *Hongaku shisō hihan*; idem, *Hihan Bukkyō*; Ishii, op. cit. For a collection of critical essays on Critical Buddhism, see Jamie Hubbard and Paul L. Swanson, eds., *Pruning the Bodhi Tree: The Storm over Critical Buddhism*. For a treatment of Tendai *hongaku* thought, see Jacqueline I. Stone, *Original Enlightenment and the Transformation of Medieval Japanese Buddhism*.

25. William R. LaFleur, *The Karma of Words: Buddhism and the Literary Arts in Medieval Japan*, p. 93.

26. Bu-ston (1290–1364), a Tibetan historian of Buddhism, gathered together from the various texts the Buddha's "intentions" for teaching the *tathāgatagarbha* doctrine "in order to (1) eliminate despair and generate effort, giving the practitioner hope of attaining liberation; (2) eliminate pride and produce respect for others; (3) eliminate absolutistic reifications and nihilistic repudiations and produce wisdom." See Robert A. F. Thurman, "Tathāgata-Garbha," in *The Encyclopedia of Religion*, vol. 14, pp. 354–56.

27. For the Senika heresy, along with "mind's eternity and form's perishability," see *S*, "Bendōwa" (Question-and-Answer 10). See also *S*, "Busshō," "Sokushin zebutsu," and "Shizen biku." For the naturalist heresy, see *S*, "Shinjin gakudō" and "Shizen biku."

28. As for various rival theories of Tendai *hongaku* thought, see Stone, op. cit., pp. 55–94.

29. Nakamura Hajime, *Ways of Thinking of Eastern Peoples: India, China, Tibet, Japan*, pp. 350–406, where he discusses absolute phenomenalism as a feature of the Japanese way of thinking.

30. *S*, "Kokū."

Chapter 4. The Reason of Words and Letters

1. Huntington summarizes the Mādhyamika philosophy of language, by way of delineating the history of the Western interpretations of Mādhyamika thought, in his op. cit., pp. 25–67. See also Mervyn Sprung's short essay, "Non-Cognitive Language in Mādhyamika Buddhism," in Leslie S. Kawamura and Keith Scott, eds., *Buddhist Thought and Asian Civilization*, pp. 241–53.

2. Wood, op. cit.

3. *S*, "Bukkyō" (47).

4. Dōgen, *Tenzo kyōkun.*

5. *S*, "Keisei sanshoku." See also *S*, "Mujō seppō."

6. This view, derived from Asaṅga's *Mahāyāna-saṃgraha* (*She ta-ch'eng lun*) 4, also appears in *S*, "Genjō kōan."

7. *S*, "Genjō kōan."

8. Kim, *Eihei Dōgen*, pp. 199–200.

9. *S*, "Sansuikyō."

10. Kim, "'The Reason of Words and Letters': Dōgen and Kōan Language," in LaFleur, op. cit., p. 59.

11. *S*, "Dōtoku."

12. *S*, "Dōtoku."

13. The following presentation on the seven headings is adapted for the present work, with minor changes, in an abridged version, from my original essay cited above in note 10, by permission of University of Hawaii Press.

In this connection, let me acknowledge my indebtedness especially to Kaga-mishima Genryū, *Dōgen zenji to in'yō kyōten-goroku no kenkyū*, and Terada Tōru, op. cit. Both Kagamishima and Terada, however, do not sufficiently delve into the intrinsic relationship between linguistic activity and Zen practice in Dōgen's religion. My investigation and analysis are a modest attempt to go beyond Kaga-mishima and Terada by showing that linguistic activity is an indispensable part of salvific realization demanded by the logic of Dōgen's Zen.

14. *S*, "Sokushin zebutsu."

15. *S*, "Bukkyō" (34).

16. To illustrate just one example: The two Chinese characters *katachi* ("form") and *gotoku* ("like") in *kedashi musō zammai no katachi mangetsu no gotoku naruo motte nari* (". . . . because the formless *samādhi* has its form just like the full moon") are combined together and rendered as *gyō-nyo* ("to embody thusness," "to form thusness," "form-thusness"). The quite ordinary characters meaning nothing more than "a form just like" are dramatically altered in their signification; as a result, form is no longer likeness but thusness itself. See *S*, "Busshō."

17. Abe Masao's discussion of Buddha-nature in his *A Study of Dōgen*, pp. 35–76.

18. *S*, "Zenki."

19. *S*, "Kembutsu."

20. *S*, "Juki."

21. *S*, "Kaiin zammai."

22. *S*, "Kūge."

23. *S*, "Kūge."

24. *S*, "Tsuki."

25. *S*, "Baika."

26. *S*, "Baika."

27. *S*, "Uji."

28. *S*, "Uji."

29. *Vajracchedikā-prajñāpāramitā sūtra*. See Edward Conze, *Buddhist Wisdom Books*, pp. 17–74. D. T. Suzuki interprets Zen from the perspective of this tradition in terms of *sokuhi no ronri*, "the logic of identity-and-difference."

30. *S*, "Busshō."

31. *S*, "Sansuikyō."

32. *S*, "Uji."

33. Although I use "intra-dharmic" and "inter-dharmic," I do so advisedly, with full awareness that these expressions are at best only an approximation.

34. Regarding reflexivity in religion, see Barbara A. Baccock, "Reflexivity," in Mircea Eliade, ed., *The Encyclopedia of Religion*, vol. 12, pp. 234–38. See also Hilary Lawson, *Reflexivity*, for an instructive discussion of the subject matter in the modern and postmodern philosophical context.

35. *S*, "Uji."

36. *S*, "Sansuikyō."

37. *S*, "Zenki."

38. *S*, "Kattō."

39. *S*, "Shohō jissō."

40. *S*, "Muchū setsumu."

41. *S*, "Gabyō."

42. *S*, "Shisho."

43. Takasaki Jikidō and Umehara Takeshi, *Kobutsu no menehi: Dōgen*, pp. 43–52.

44. S, "Busshō."

45. S, "Tashintsū."

46. S, "Kattō."

47. S, "Kokyō."

48. See Kagamishima, op. cit., pp. 69–71.

Chapter 5. Meditation as Authentic Thinking

1. Carl Bielefeldt, *Dōgen's Manuals of Zen Meditation*, pp. 5–7 on "Dōgen Zen."

2. Ishii, op. cit.; Matsumoto Shirō, "The Meaning of 'Zen,'" in Hubbard and Swanson, eds., *Pruning the Bodhi Tree*, pp. 242–50.

3. Edward Conze, *Buddhism: Its Essence and Development*, p. 40 and pp. 161–62; Mircea Eliade, *Yoga: Immortality and Freedom*, pp. 173–77.

4. Izutsu Toshihiko, *Towards a Philosophy of Zen Buddhism*, pp. 147–60.

5. Abe Masao, *Zen and Western Thought*, p. 24.

6. Ibid., p. 112.

7. Ibid., p.117. Abe discusses the notion of nonthinking primarily in the context of chapter 4, "Zen and Western Thought" (pp. 83–120).

8. S, "Ippyakuhachi hōmyōmon."

9. S, "Zazenshin." Cf. This is similar in thinking to Dōgen's view of Buddha-nature that is said to "have already arrived" (*kishi*) instead of "if it arrives" (*nyakushi*). See S, "Busshō."

10. S, "Daigo," "Kōmyō," and so forth. See also "Mitsugo" for Dōgen's notion of intimacy (*mitsu*; *shimmitsu*).

11. See chapter 1, note 10 above and chapter 6, section 8 below.

12. S, "Hotsu bodaishin." See also S, "Shinjin gakudō" and "Sesshin sesshō."

13. S, "Shinjin gakudō."

14. S, "Sanjūshichihon bodaibumpō."

15. S, "Hotsu mujōshin."

16. S, "Sokushin zebutsu."

17. S, "Tsuki."

18. *S*, "Hotsu mujōshin."

19. On "the attainment of cessation" in the Theravāda tradition, see Winston L. King, *Theravāda Meditation: The Buddhist Transformation of Yoga*, pp. 103–15; Paul J. Griffiths, *On Being Mindless: Buddhist Meditation and the Mind-Body Problem*, pp. 1–42.

20. Griffiths, op. cit., pp. 27–31.

21. King, op. cit., p. 105. He writes: "If all thinking and feeling completely stop, how can it be an 'experience'? It cannot be such *during* the cessation itself." See also pp. 108–15.

22. *S*, "Zazenshin."

23. Eliade, op. cit., p. 339: "As a developed spiritual technique (we are not discussing its possible 'origins') Yoga cannot possibly be confused with shamanism or classed among the techniques of ecstasy. The goal of classic Yoga remains perfect *autonomy*, enstasis, while shamanism is characterized by its desperate effort to attain the 'condition of a spirit,' to accomplish ecstatic flight. Nevertheless, there is a definite point where Yoga and shamanism meet. They meet in 'emergence from time' and the abolition of history."

24. See Gadjin M. Nagao, "What Remains in *Śūnyatā*: A Yogācāra Interpretation of Emptiness," in his *Mādhyamika and Yogācāra: A Study of Mahāyāna Philosophies*, pp. 51–60.

25. In *The Zen Doctrine of No Mind*, D. T. Suzuki employs "the Unconscious" (not a psychological but a metaphysical notion, as Suzuki emphasizes) for the notions of no-thought (*wu-nien*; *munen*) and no-mind (*wu-hsin*; *mushin*) in the sixth patriarch Hui-neng's *Platform Sūtra*, and thus writes, for example: "[The Unconscious] extricates itself, if we can say so, from its own contradictory nature and is itself" (p. 128); "If a thought is awakened and any form of functioning is recognized, there is a discrimination, an attachment, a deviation from the path of the Unconscious" (p. 74, note 2). See also idem, *Living by Zen*, pp. 29–30.

26. *S*, "Ango."

27. *S*, "Hosshō."

28. *S*, "Kokū."

29. *S*, "Kattō." I use the terms "limitations" and "possibilities" descriptively; only when they are misused or abused do they become delusions and defilements. Practitioners work with their limitations and possibilities in and through karmic consciousness (*gosshiki*) in which they are intertwined and interpenetrated like vines (*kattō*).

30. For this and related issues, see Bernard Faure, *The Rhetoric of Immediacy: A Cultural Critique of Chan/Zen Buddhism.*

31. *S,* "Shinfukatoku."

32. *S,* "Shinfukatoku."

33. On recent discussion of apophatic mysticism and negative theology, see: Harold Coward and Toby Foshay, eds., *Derrida and Negative Theology*; Robert K. C. Forman, ed., *The Problem of Pure Consciousness: Mysticism and Philosophy*; Steven T. Katz, ed., *Mysticism and Philosophical Analysis*; idem, ed., *Mysticism and Religious Traditions*; idem, ed., *Mysticism and Language.*

34. Kim, *Eihei Dōgen,* pp. 134–37.

35. *S,* "Immo."

36. To put it another way, the answer is always already in the question.

37. *S,* "Keisei sanshoku." See also "Genjō kōan," "Juki," "Hakujushi," and "Kūge." Surprisingly agnostic and skeptical as it may seem, it is after all quite different from the modern/postmodern varieties.

38. *S,* "Sanjūshichihon bodaibumpō."

39. The eightfold right path is divided into these three divisions: (1) morality (right speech, right action, and right livelihood), (2) meditation (right effort, right mindfulness, and right concentration), and (3) wisdom (right understanding and right thought). Morality (*kai*), meditation (*jō*), and wisdom (*e*) are called "three forms of learning" (*sangaku*)—or, more appropriately, the three forms of praxis.

40. *S,* "Kaiin zammai."

41. Bielefeldt, op. cit. These summary acounts are given in my review of Bieflefeldt's book, in *The Eastern Buddhistm* (New Series), vol. 23, no.1 (September 1990), pp.141–46. In addition to the popular text of the *Fukan zazengi* (circa 1243), there are the three other meditation manuals of the same period: The *Shōbōgenzō*, "Zazenshin" (1242) and "Zazengi" (1243), and *Bendōhō* (1245) that includes a section on meditation.

42. Bielefeldt, op. cit., pp. 133–60 offers his interpretation of nonthinking.

43. To cite just a few: Robert M. Gimmelo, "Mysticism and Meditation" in Katz, ed., *Mysticism and Philosophical Analysis,* pp. 170–99: "In Buddhism, . . . meditation has always been one, if not *the,* central form of praxis." In the Theravāda tradition, Rahula, op. cit., p. 68: "[*Samatha*] is not essential for the realization of Nirvāṇa . . . [*Vipassanā*] lead[s] to the complete liberation of mind, to the realization of the Ultimate Truth, Nirvāṇa." Nyanaponika Thera, *The Heart of Buddhist Meditation,* p. 102: "the Development of Tranquility or the meditative Absorptions,

are only means to an end, and cannot lead, by themselves, to the highest goal of liberation which is attainable only through Insight." As for the early Buddhist view of the issue, see Hirakawa Akira, *A History of Indian Buddhism: From Śākyamuni to Early Mahāyāna*, pp. 217–19.

44. Terada, op. cit., pp. 145–46.

Chapter 6. Radical Reason: *Dōri*

1. These issues are discussed in debates between constructivists and non-constructivists in the work by Katz and Forman, cited before in chapter 5, note 33. See also Richard H. Jones, *Mysticism Examined: Philosophical Inquiries into Mysticism*. Rgarding altered states of consciousness, see Charles T. Tart, ed., *Altered States of Consciousness: A Book of Readings*, which includes a pioneering treatment of the subject, Arthur J. Deikman's "Deautomatization and the Mystic Experience," in *Psychiatry*, vol. 29 (1966), pp. 324–38.

2. Martin Heidegger, *An Introduction to Metaphysics*, pp. 98–164.

3. Notable among works in this area is: Carl Olson, *Zen and the Art of Postmodern Philosophy: Two Paths of Liberation from the Representational Mode of Thinking*.

4. A. C. Graham, *Disputers of the Tao*, pp. 13–15, 18, 362–63.

5. Helmut Wilhelm, *Heaven, Earth, and Man in the Book of Changes: Seven Eranos Lectures*, p. 72.

6. Roger T. Ames, "Chinese Rationality: An Oxymoron?" *Journal of Indian Council of Philosophical Research*, vol. 9, no. 2 (January–April 1992), pp. 95–119.

7. As for this distinction, see David L. Hall and Roger T. Ames, *Thinking through Confucius*, p. 16 and pp. 131–38. Graham also offers a similar distinction in terms of "analytic thinking" and "correlative thinking" in his op. cit. In this connection, see also idem, *Unreason within Reason: Essays on the Outskirts of Rationality*.

8. Nakamura, op. cit., p. 246.

9. For a useful summary of the evolution of the idea of *dōri* in medieval Japanese thought, see Watsuji Tetsurō, *Nihon rinri shisō-shi*, vol. 1, pp. 319–49. Regarding the relation of the notion of *dōri* to the Kamakura Buddhist leaders such as Shinran, Dōgen, and Nichiren, see Tamura, op. cit., pp. 234–55.

10. *S*, "Busshō."

11. See note 33 below.

12. Kim, *Eihei Dōgen*, pp. 126–33.

13. *S*, "Jinshin inga."

14. *S*, "Gyōji" II.

15. *S*, "Sanjigō."

16. *S*, "Daishugyō." Elsewhere in "Shoaku makusa," Dōgen calls cause "wondrous cause" (*myōin*) and "buddha cause" (*butsuin*), whereas effect "wondrous effect" (*myōka*) and "buddha effect" (*bukka*).

17. On this hymn, see Kim, *Eihei Dōgen*, pp. 224–29.

18. *S*, "Shoaku makusa."

19. *S*, "Shoaku makusa."

20. Regarding *hōni dōri* and its significance in Kamakura Buddhism, see Tamura, op. cit., pp. 234–55.

21. Ueda Yoshifumi and Dennis Hirota, *Shinran: An Introduction to His Thought*, pp. 272–73. See also ibid., pp. 176–78.

22. *S*, "Gyōbutsu iigi."

23. *S*, "Shōji."

24. E.g., see *S*, "Jinshin inga" and "Shizen biku."

25. *S*, "Shizen biku." For widely diverse views of nature and naturalness within the Taoist tradition, including one of Kuo Hsiang's (d. 312) interpretations in his commentary on the *Chuang-tzu*, a view very similar to the naturalist heresy in Dōgen's writings, see Mori Mikisaburō, *Mu no shisō: Rōsō shisō no keifu*.

26. Dōgen, *Bendōhō*.

27. *S*, "Jinshin inga."

28. *S*, "Kūge."

29. *S*, "Hosshō."

30. *S*, "Hosshō."

31. *S*, "Hosshō."

32. *S*, "Hosshō."

33. In this connection, let me touch on a rather unusual illustration, which I hope is not entirely off the mark in the present context. Perhaps no two spheres of human knowledge could seem more disparate and heterogeneous than esotericism and modern science—more specifically, say, alchemy and chemistry. One is dismissed as a dubious proto- or prescientific superstition and the other reputed as a hallmark of scientific rationality. But note the following statement by Elgin: "Men are not credulous because they believe anything, but because they believe

anything *within reason*: a man, that is, will be credulous according to his time. The language of Alchemy is, to the modern observer, a transparent nonsense. . . . This, however, is not equivalent to merely noting that the language of Alchemy is unintelligible, for although the language of science is largely unintelligible to the nonscientist, it is not ipso facto nonsense. The practice of Alchemy was rooted in a deeply sedimented sense of the terms and methods via which a thing's or an event's existence—no less than its rational accountability—was demonstrated and made observable." (Trent Elgin, "Introduction to a Hermeneutics of the Occult: Alchemy," in Edward A. Tiryakian, ed., *On the Margin of the Visible: Sociology, the Esoteric, and the Occult*, pp. 323–50. This quotation appears on p. 332; emphasis original.) The issue has to do with not rationality against irrationality but one form of rationality against another. Cf. Hakamaya Noriaki, "Scholarship as Criticism," in Hubbard and Swanson, eds., op. cit., pp. 113–44.

On issues of rationality, Toulmin, op. cit. is instructive. Toulmin's thesis is strikingly similar to the Buddhist emphasis on skillfulness in thought, speech, and action to cope with challenging situations. Yet Dōgen's view of reason points to the direction that is far broader and more fundamental than Toulmin's with respect to understanding and criticism. A similar observation may be made with respect to Elgin's thesis as well.

34. In light of these observations, Dōgen's criticism, despite his occasionally invective and unwarrantable tones and rhetoric, was essentially much kinder and gentler, as compared with Critical Buddhists', precisely because it originated in his hermeneutic method that excludes nothing from its field of vision. Critical Buddhists on the other hand lack a hermeneutic sensitivity by which their criticism may be better informed and tempered; consequently, they fail to negotiate what remains outside the horizon of their intellect, as the practice of the Way. Their intellectualism, as a result, varies from Dōgen's that was egalitarian at the core, for all his seeming or presumed elitism and purism.

35. *S*, "Gabyō."

36. *S*, "Baika."

37. *S*, "Gabyō."

38. This verbal use of the word *gato* occurs elsewhere in *S*, "Shinjin gakudō," "Baika," and "Zammai ō zammai." Dōgen also uses verbs such as *ga su* (from *ga*, "picture") and *zu su* (from *zu*, "picture," "drawing").

39. *S*, "Gabyō."

40. Dōgen, *Tenzo kyōkun*.

41. See John C. Gilmour, *Picturing the World* that gives instructive analyses of various issues involved—especially, pp. 52–130 regarding picture and language.

42. *S*, "Immo."

43. *S*, "Immo."

Postscript

1. *S*, "Hosshō."

2. *S*, "Hosshō."

Bibliography

Abe Masao. *A Study of Dōgen: His Philosophy and Religion.* Ed. Steven Heine. Albany: State University of New York Press, 1992.

————. *Zen and Western Thought.* Ed. William R. LaFleur. Honolulu: University of Hawaii Press, 1985.

Ames, Roger T. "Chinese Rationality: An Oxymoron?" *Journal of Indian Council of Philosophical Research*, vol. 9, no. 2 (January–April 1992), pp. 95–119.

App, Urs, trans. *Master Yunmen: From the Record of the Chan Master "Gate of the Clouds."* New York & London: Kōdansha International, 1994.

Austin, J. L. *How to Do Things with Words.* Ed. J. O. Urmson. New York: Oxford University Press, 1965.

Baccock, Barbara A. "Reflexivity." Mircea Eliade, ed., *The Encyclopedia of Religion*, vol. 12. New York: Macmillan, 1987, pp. 234–38.

Bielefeldt, Carl. *Dōgen's Manuals of Zen Meditation.* Berkeley & Los Angeles: University of California Press, 1988.

Bodiford, William M. *Sōtō Zen in Medieval Japan.* Honolulu: University of Hawaii Press, 1993.

Cleary, Thomas, and J. C. Cleary, trans. *The Blue Cliff Record.* 3 vols. Boulder & London: Shambhala, 1977.

Conze, Edward. *Buddhism: Its Essence and Development.* Harper Torchbook. New York: Harper & Brothers, 1951.

————, trans. *Buddhist Wisdom Books.* New York & San Francisco: Harper & Row, 1958.

Cook, Francis H. *Sounds of Valley Streams: Enlightenment in Dōgen's Zen, Translation of Nine Essays from Shōbōgenzō.* Albany: State University of New York Press, 1989.

Coward, Harrold, and Toby Foshay, eds. *Derrida and Negative Theology*. Albany: State University of New York Press, 1992.

Dōgen. *Bendōhō. Dōgen zenji zenshū*, vol. 2. Ed. Ōkubo Dōshū. Tokyo: Chikuma shobō, 1970, pp. 313–319.

———. *Eihei kōroku (Dōgen oshō kōroku). Dōgen zenji zenshū*, vol. 2. Ed. Ōkubo Dōshū. Tokyo: Chikuma shobō, 1970, pp. 7–200.

———. *Fukan zazengi. Dōgen zenji zenshū*, vol. 2. Ed. Ōkubo Dōshū. Tokyo: Chikuma shobō, 1970, pp. 3–5 and 165–166.

———. *Shōbōgenzō. Dōgen zenji zenshū*, vol. 1. Ed. Ōkubo Dōshū. Tokyo: Chikuma shobō, 1969; *Dōgen*. 2 vols. *Nihon shisō taikei* 12 and 13. Ed. Terada Tōru and Mizuno Yaoko. Tokyo: Iwanami shoten, 1970 and 1972.

———. *Tenzo kyōkun. Dōgen zenji zenshū*, vol. 2. Ed. Ōkubo Dōshū. Tokyo: Chikuma shobō, 1970, pp. 295–303.

Elgin, Trent. "Introduction to a Hermeneutics of the Occult: Alchemy." Edward A. Tiryakian, ed., *On the Margin of the Visible: Sociology, the Esoteric, and the Occult*. New York & London: Wiley, 1974, pp. 323–50.

Eliade, Mircea. *Yoga: Immortality and Freedom*. Trans. Willard R. Trask. New York: Bollingen Foundation/Pantheon, 1958.

Faure, Bernard. *Chan Insights and Oversights: An Epistemological Critique of the Chan Tradition*. Princeton: Princeton University Press, 1993.

———. *The Rhetoric of Immediacy: A Cultural Critique of Chan/Zen Buddhism*. Princeton: Princeton University Press, 1991.

Fingarette, Herbert. *Confucius—The Secular as Sacred*. New York & London: Harper & Row, 1972.

Forman, Robert K. C., ed. *The Problem of Pure Consciousness: Mysticism and Philosophy*. New York & Oxford: Oxford University Press, 1990.

Fu, Charles Wei-hsun, and Steven Heine, eds. *Japan in Traditional and Postmodern Perspectives*. Albany: State University of New York Press, 1995.

Gilmour, John C. *Picturing the World*. Albany: State University of New York Press, 1986.

Gimmelo, Robert M. "Mysticism and Meditation." Steven T. Katz, ed., *Mysticism and Philosophical Analysis*. New York: Oxford University Press, 1978, pp. 170–99.

Graham, A. C. *Disputers of the Tao: Philosophical Argument in Ancient China*. La Salle: Open Court, 1989.

———. *Unreason within Reason: Essays on the Outskirts of Rationality.* La Salle: Open Court, 1992.

Gregory, Peter G., ed. *Sudden and Gradual: Approaches to Enlightenment in Chinese Thought.* Honolulu: University of Hawaii Press, 1987.

Griffiths, Paul J. *On Being Mindless: Buddhist Meditation and the Mind-Body Problem.* La Salle: Open Court, 1986.

Hakamaya Noriaki. *Hihan Bukkyō.* Tokyo: Daizō shuppan, 1990.

———. *Hongaku shisō hihan.* Tokyo: Daizō shuppan, 1989.

———. "Scholarship as Criticism." Jamie Hubbard and Paul L. Swanson, eds., *Pruning the Bodhi Tree: The Storm over Critical Buddhism.* Honolulu: University of Hawaii Press, 1997, pp. 113–44.

Hall, David L., and Roger T. Ames. *Thinking through Confucius.* Albany: State University of New York Press, 1987.

Hayashima Kyōshō and Takasaki Jikidō, eds. *Bukkyō-Indo shisō jiten.* Tokyo: Shunjūsha, 1987.

Heidegger, Martin. *An Introduction to Metaphysics.* Trans. R. Manheim. New Haven: Yale University Press, 1959.

Heine, Steven. "Critical Buddhism and Dōgen's *Shōbōgenzō*: The Debate over the Seventy-five-Fascicle and Twelve-Fascicle Texts." Jamie Hubbard and Paul L. Swanson, eds., *Pruning the Bodhi Tree: The Storm over Critical Buddhism.* Honolulu: University of Hawaii Press, 1997, pp. 251–85.

———. *Dōgen and the Kōan Tradition: A Tale of Two Shōbōgenzō Texts.* Albany: State University of New York Press, 1994.

———. *The Zen Poetry of Dōgen: Verses from the Mountain of Eternal Peace.* Boston: Tuttle, 1997.

Heine, Steven, and Dale S. Wright, eds. *The Kōan: Texts and Contexts in Zen Buddhism.* New York: Oxford University Press, 2000.

Heisig, James W., and John Maraldo, eds. *Rude Awakenings: Zen, the Kyoto School, and the Question of Nationalism.* Honolulu: University of Hawaii Press, 1994.

Hirakawa Akira. *A History of Indian Buddhism: From Śākyamuni to Early Mahāyāna.* Trans. and ed. Paul Groner. Honolulu: University of Hawaii Press, 1990.

Hisamatsu Shin'ichi. "The Characteristics of Oriental Nothingness." *Philosophical Studies of Japan* 2 (1960), pp. 80–85.

Hubbard, Jamie, and Paul L. Swanson, eds. *Pruning the Bodhi Tree: The Storm over Critical Buddhism.* Honolulu: University of Hawaii Press, 1997.

Huntington, C. W., Jr., with Geshé Namgyal Wangchen. *The Emptiness of Emptiness: An Introduction to Early Indian Mādhyamika.* Honolulu: University of Hawaii Press, 1989.

Ishii Shūdō. "Recent Trends in Dōgen Studies." *Komazawa daigaku zen kenkyūjo nempō*, no. 1 (March 1990), pp. 219–64.

Ives, Christopher. "Ethical Pitfalls in Imperial Zen and Nishida Philosophy: Ichikawa Hakugen's Critique." James W. Heisig and John Maraldo, eds., *Rude Awakenings: Zen, the Kyoto School, and the Question of Nationalism.* Honolulu: University of Hawaii Press, 1994, pp. 16–39.

Izutsu Toshihiko. *Towards a Philosophy of Zen Buddhism.* Tehran: Imperial Iranian Academy of Philosophy, 1977.

Jones, Richard H. *Mysticism Examined: Philosophical Inquiries into Mysticism.* Albany: State University of New York Press, 1993.

Kagamishima Genryū. *Dōgen zenji to in'yō kyōten-goroku no kenkyū.* Tokyo: Mokujisha, 1974.

Kagamishima Genryū and Suzuki Kakuzen, eds. *Jūnikanbon Shōbōgenzō no shomondai.* Tokyo: Daizō shuppan, 1991.

Kagamishima Genryū and Tamaki Kōshirō, eds. *Kōza Dōgen.* 7 vols. Tokyo: Shunjūsha, 1978–1981.

Katz, Steven T., ed. *Mysticism and Language.* New York & Oxford: Oxford University Press, 1992.

———, ed. *Mysticism and Philosophical Analysis.* New York: Oxford University Press, 1978.

———, ed. *Mysticism and Religious Traditions.* New York & Oxford: Oxford University Press, 1983.

Kawamura, Leslie S., ed. *The Bodhisattva Doctrine in Buddhism.* Waterloo: Wilfrid Laurier University Press, 1981.

Kim, Hee-Jin. *Eihei Dōgen: Mystical Realist.* Boston: Wisdom Publications, 2004. The reissue of *Dōgen Kigen: Mystical Realist* (Tucson: University of Arizona Press, 1975 and 1987).

———, trans. *Flowers of Emptiness: Selections from Dōgen's Shōbōgenzō.* Lewiston: Mellen, 1985.

———. "'The Reason of Words and Letters': Dōgen and Kōan Language." William R. LaFleur, ed., *Dōgen Studies.* Honolulu: University of Hawaii Press, 1985, pp. 54–82.

————. "Review: *Dōgen's Manuals of Zen Meditation* by Carl Bielefeldt." *The Eastern Buddhist* (New Series), vol. 23, no. 1 (September 1990), pp. 141–46.

King, Winston L. *Theravāda Meditation: The Buddhist Transformation of Yoga.* University Park & London: Pennsylvania State University Press, 1980.

LaFleur, William R., ed. *Dōgen Studies.* Honolulu: University of Hawaii Press, 1985.

————. *The Karma of Words: Buddhism and the Literary Arts in Medieval Japan.* Berkeley & Los Angeles: University of California Press, 1983.

Lau, D. C., trans. *Lao Tzu: Tao Te Ching.* Harmondsworth: Penguin, 1963.

Lawson, Hilary. *Reflexivity: The Postmodern Predicament.* La Salle: Open Court, 1985.

Lopez, Donald S., Jr., ed. *Buddhist Hermeneutics.* Honolulu: University of Hawaii Press, 1988.

————, ed. *Curators of the Buddha: The Study of Buddhism under Colonialism.* Chicago & London: University of Chicago Press, 1995.

Maraldo, John C. "Questioning Nationalism Now and Then: A Critical Approach to Zen and the Kyoto School." James W. Heisig and John Maraldo, eds., *Rude Awakenings: Zen, the Kyoto School, and the Question of Nationalism.* Honolulu: University of Hawaii Press, 1994, pp. 333–62.

Matsumoto Shirō. *Engi to kū: nyoraizō shisō hihan.* Tokyo: Daizō shuppan, 1989.

————. "The Meaning of 'Zen.'" Jamie Hubbard and Paul L. Swanson, eds., *Pruning the Bodhi Tree: The Storm over Critical Buddhism.* Honolulu: University of Hawaii Press, 1997, pp. 242–50.

McFarland, H. Neill. *The Rush Hour of the Gods: A Study of New Religious Movements in Japan.* New York: Macmillan, 1967.

McRae, John R. *The Northern School and the Formation of Early Ch'an Buddhism.* Honolulu: University of Hawaii Press, 1986.

Mori Mikisaburō. *Mu no shisō: Rōsō shisō no keifu.* Tokyo: Kōdansha, 1969.

Nagao Gadjin M. *Mādhyamika and Yogācāra: A Study of Mahāyāna Philosophies.* Ed. and trans. L. S. Kawamura. Albany: State University of New York Press, 1991.

Nakamura Hajime. *Ways of Thinking of Eastern Peoples: India, China, Tibet, Japan.* Honolulu: East-West Center Press, 1964.

Nara Yasuaki, ed. *Budda kara Dōgen e: Bukkyō tōron-shū.* Tokyo: Tokyo shoseki, 1992.

Nyanaponika Thera. *The Heart of Buddhist Meditation.* London: Rider, 1962.

Ōkubo Dōshū, ed. *Dōgen zenji zenshū.* 2 vols. Tokyo: Chikuma shobō, 1969 and 1970.

Olson, Carl. *Zen and the Art of Postmodern Philosophy: Two Paths of Liberation from the Representational Mode of Thinking.* Albany: State University of New York Press, 2000.

Ōta Kyūki. "Hossō kyōgaku to Dōgen." Kagamishima Genryū and Tamaki Kōshirō, eds., *Bukkyō kyōgaku to Dōgen. Kōza Dōgen,* vol. 6. Tokyo: Shunjūsha, 1980, pp. 77–102.

Pascal, Blaise. *Pascal's Pensées.* Everyman's Library 874. New York: Dutton, 1932.

Proudfoot, Wayne. *Religious Experience.* Berkeley & Los Angeles: University of California Press, 1985.

Pye, Michael. *Skillful Means: A Concept in Mahāyāna Buddhism.* London: Duckworth, 1978.

Rahula, Walpola. *What the Buddha Taught.* New York: Grove, 1962.

Sharf, Robert H. "Experience." Marc C. Taylor, ed., *Critical Terms for Religious Studies.* Chicago & London: University of Chicago Press, 1998, pp. 94–116.

————. "Whose Zen? Zen Nationalism Revisited." James W. Heisig and John Maraldo, eds., *Rude Awakenings: Zen, the Kyoto School, and the Question of Nationalism.* Honolulu: University of Hawaii Press, 1994, pp. 40–51.

————. "The Zen of Japanese Nationalism." Donald S. Lopez, Jr., ed., *Curators of the Buddha: Study of Buddhism under Colonialism.* Chicago & London: University of Chicago Press, 1995, pp. 107–60.

Sprung, Mervyn. "Non-cognitive Language in Mādhyamika Buddhism." Leslie S. Kawamura and Keith Scott, eds., *Buddhist Thought and Asian Civilization: Essays in Honor of Herbert V. Guenther on His Sixtieth Birthday.* Emeryville, CA: Dharma Publishing, 1977, pp. 241–53.

Stone, Jaqueline I. *Original Enlightenment and the Transformation of Medieval Japanese Buddhism.* Honolulu: University of Hawaii Press, 1999.

Suzuki, D. T. *Living by Zen.* New York: Weiser, 1972.

————. *Zen and Japanese Culture.* New York: Pantheon, 1959.

————. *The Zen Doctrine of No Mind: The Significance of the Sūtra of Hui-neng (Wei-Lang).* New York: Weiser, 1972.

Takasaki Jikidō and Umehara Takeshi. *Kobutsu no manebi: Dōgen. Bukkyō no shisō* 11. Tokyo: Kadokawa shoten, 1969.

Tamura Yoshirō. *Kamakura shin-Bukkyō shisō no kenkyū.* Kyoto: Heirakuji shoten, 1965.

Tart, Charles T., ed. *Altered States of Consciousness: A Book of Readings.* New York & London: Wiley, 1969.

Taylor, Mark C., ed. *Critical Terms for Religious Studies.* Chicago & London: University of Chicago Press, 1998.

Terada Tōru. *Dōgen no gengo uchū.* Tokyo: Iwanami shoten, 1974.

Terada Tōru and Mizuno Yaoko, eds. *Dōgen.* 2 vols. *Nihon shisō taikei* 12 and 13. Tokyo: Iwanami shoten, 1970 and 1972.

Thurman, Robert A. F., trans. *The Holy Teaching of Vimalakīrti: A Mahāyāna Scripture.* University Park & London: Pennsylvania State University Press, 1976.

———. "Tathāgata-Garbha." Mircea Eliade, ed., *The Encyclopedia of Religion,* vol. 14. New York: Macmillan, 1987, pp. 354–56.

Tiryakian, Edward A., ed. *On the Margin of the Visible: Sociology, the Esoteric, and the Occult.* New York & London: Wiley, 1974.

Toulmin, Stephen. *Human Understanding: The Collective Use and Evolution of Concepts.* Princeton: Princeton University Press, 1972.

Ueda Yoshifumi and Dennis Hirota. *Shinran: An Introduction to His Thought.* Kyoto: Hongwanji International Center, 1989.

Waddell, Norman, and Abe Masao, trans. *The Heart of Dōgen's Shōbōgenzō.* Albany: State University of New York Press, 2002.

Waley, Arthur, trans. *The Analects of Confucius.* New York: Vintage, 1938.

Watsuji Tetsurō. *Nihon rinri shisō-shi.* 2 vols. Tokyo: Iwanami shoten, 1952.

Wilhelm, Hellmut. *Heaven, Earth, and Man in the Book of Changes: Seven Eranos Lectures.* Seattle & London: University of Washington Press, 1977.

Wood, Thomas E. *Nāgārjunian Disputations: A Philosophical Journey through an Indian Looking Glass.* Honolulu: University of Hawaii Press, 1994.

Yuasa Yasuo. *The Body: Toward an Eastern Mind-Body Theory.* Ed. Thomas P. Kasulis; trans. Nagatomo Shigenori and Thomas P. Kasulis. Albany: State University of New York Press, 1987.

Index